WHAT PEOPLE ARE SAYING

Spellbound

Spellbound *provides readers with crucial information that is clearly and compellingly presented. Marcia Montenegro writes from experience but also appeals to evidence and biblical truth. Parents will appreciate* Spellbound's *candid and straightforward approach.*

—ROBERT VELARDE
FOCUS ON THE FAMILY
AUTHOR, *THE LION, THE WITCH, AND THE BIBLE*

With the growth of occultism in culture and even in the church, Marcia's book Spellbound *is a must read for families.*

—L. L. (DON) VEINOT JR.
PRESIDENT, MIDWEST CHRISTIAN OUTREACH, INC.

SPELLBOUND

MARCIA MONTENEGRO

LIFE JOURNEY®

Bringing Home the Message for Life

COOK COMMUNICATIONS MINISTRIES
Colorado Springs, Colorado • Paris, Ontario
KINGSWAY COMMUNICATIONS LTD
Eastbourne, England

Life Journey® is an imprint of
Cook Communications Ministries, Colorado Springs, CO 80918
Cook Communications, Paris, Ontario
Kingsway Communications, Eastbourne, England

SPELLBOUND
© 2006 Marcia Montenegro

The Web addresses (URLs) recommended throughout this book are solely
offered as a resource to the reader. The citation of these Web sites does not
in any way imply an endorsement on the part of the author or the publisher,
nor does the author or publisher vouch for their content for the life of this
book.

Cover Design: BMB Design

First Printing, 2006
Printed in the United States of America

1 2 3 4 5 6 7 8 9 10 Printing/Year 10 09 08 07 06

Unless otherwise noted, Scripture quotations are taken from the *New
American Standard Bible*, © Copyright 1960, 1995 by The Lockman
Foundation. Used by permission. Scripture quotations marked NIV are taken
from the *Holy Bible, New International Version*®. NIV®. Copyright © 1973,
1978, 1984 by International Bible Society. Used by permission of
Zondervan. All rights reserved; NLT are taken from the *Holy Bible, New
Living Translation*, copyright © 1996. Used by permission of Tyndale
House Publishers, Inc., Wheaton, Illinois 60189. All rights reserved; ESV are
taken from *The Holy Bible, English Standard Version*. Copyright © 2000;
2001 by Crossway Bibles, a division of Good News Publishers. Used by permission. All rights reserved; and NKJV are taken from the New King James
Version. Copyright © 1982 by Thomas Nelson, Inc. Used by permission. All
rights reserved. Italics in Scripture have been added by the author for
emphasis.

ISBN-13: 978-0-7814-4360-9
ISBN-10: 0-7814-4360-1

LCCN: 2006925746

I would like to dedicate this book to my son, Geoffrey Daniel, whose patience and fortitude in transitioning from life as the son of an astrologer to life as the son of a Christian was a comfort to me, and who has continued to be a model of kindness and generosity in young adulthood.
—M.M.

Contents

PART THREE:
Talking to Your Kids about the Paranormal

ACKNOWLEDGMENTS

J would like to express my deepest appreciation to Ed Stewart for bringing the publisher and me together for this book. His role was crucial for making this book happen!

I am also grateful for the encouragement and prayers I have received for this book from my many faithful prayer partners and from Steve King, pastor of Cherrydale Baptist Church. Heartfelt thanks also go to my supporting churches and friends whose partnership in the ministry has enabled me to write this book.

Editor Mary McNeil got me excited about the need for this book, and editor Mike Nappa was extremely kind and patient in dealing with a first-time book author. I appreciate and thank both of them! Also, assistant editor Diane Gardner answered a lot of questions along the way and was very reassuring. I am grateful to all the people at Cook Communications who worked on this book.

I am indebted to Dr. Geisler and the staff at Southern Evangelical Seminary whose expertise has sharpened my ablility in forming responses to many of the issues examined in this book

My son, Geoffrey, and sister, Valerie, through their encouragement and feedback, have been extremely supportive, and I am grateful to them, not just regarding this book, but also for their significant and crucial roles in my life. All three of us took part in the journey from unbelief to faith in Christ in late 1990 and 1991.

FOREWORD

Spellbound is a great title for a great book. No movement is more pervasive and more destructive to our teen culture than witchcraft and the occult. It has permeated music and the media, cartoons and comic books, TV and radio, and the public-school classroom. Most parents don't recognize it when they see it, and even most teenagers see no harm in it. From the old TV program *Bewitched* to the current craze for Harry Potter, the last several decades have been dominated by the demonic clothed as the dramatic.

Many Christians naively thought the Star Wars series to be a Christian allegory, being totally unaware that George Lucas borrowed heavily from *Don Juan* and *Tales of Power*, novels by Carlos Castenada about a Mexican sorcerer. Indeed, even Luke Skywalker, hero of the *Star Wars* series, was a sorcerer who tapped into the Light side of the Force

(so-called "White Magic") to do supernormal feats. But as
the creator of the series, George Lucas acknowledges that
ultimately there is no difference between the Light side of
this occult Force and the Dark side ("Black Magic").

The problem in recognizing the ugly nature of the occult
and the paranormal is that it is craftily packaged in such beautiful cultural forms. We laughed at witchcraft in the *I Dream
of Jeannie* TV series in the sixties. We were entertained by it
in an exciting space drama in *Star Wars* beginning in the sev-
enties. Now our teens are spellbound by a charming young
wizard, Harry Potter. The time is overdue to expose witchcraft and the occult for what it is. And there is no one better
able to do so than a former astrologer. I know of no Christian
better trained and more in tune with the influence of this subject on our culture than Marcia Montenegro.

This book is not only clear, but it is also discerning, one
of the vanishing gifts of the contemporary Christian Church.
This is true not only of the northeastern United States, the
original home of witchcraft, but also of the western United
States from California through Colorado and Texas, which
are the current abodes of the aberrant. It is also true of the
Bible Belt, which I have come to discover after residing here
over the last quarter of a century does not have enough Bible
under its belt.

The truth is that Christianity in the United States is
about three thousand miles wide and about an inch deep.
We have just enough religion to makes us susceptible to the
occult and not enough doctrine to make us discerning.
Little wonder that the great apostle Paul spent his last years
and last letters (1 Timothy, 2 Timothy, and Titus) warning
about false doctrine. His own inspired words are well worth
pondering on this matter:

The Spirit clearly says that in later times some will
abandon the faith and follow deceiving spirits and

things taught by demons. Such teachings come through hypocritical liars, whose consciences have been seared as with a hot iron. They forbid people to marry and order them to abstain from certain foods, which God created to be received with thanksgiving by those who believe and who know the truth. (1 Timothy 4:1–3 NIV)

And in his very last recorded words, the apostle who wrote nearly half of the inspired New Testament added:

But mark this: There will be terrible times in the last days. People will be lovers of themselves, lovers of money, boastful, proud, abusive, disobedient to their parents, ungrateful, unholy, without love, unforgiving, slanderous, without self-control, brutal, not lovers of the good, treacherous, rash, conceited, lovers of pleasure rather than lovers of God—having a form of godliness but denying its power. Have nothing to do with them.... While evil men and impostors will go from bad to worse, deceiving and being deceived. (2 Timothy 3:1–5, 13 NIV)

Ideas have consequences, and demonic ideas have devilish consequences. The time for discernment is upon us. Marcia Montenegro has written a biblically based, culturally relevant, and very insightful book to help us in this discernment. Every Christian home needs it. I highly recommend *Spellbound*.

Dr. Norman L. Geisler
Dean of Southern Evangelical Seminary, Charlotte, NC

Preface

FROM VILLAIN
TO HERO

$\mathcal{I}$ have lived this book.

The beginning of my journey into the paranormal was a vivid dream I had at age eleven. In the dream, I found myself in a house searching for a playmate named Gary, a real boy I had actually played with years earlier. I went into each room calling out his name, but was unable find him. Finally, I reached a closet and opened the door. Inside, a gaggle of children acted surprised to be found and started laughing. "Is Gary here?" I called out. One by one, the children left the closet until finally it was empty. No Gary. I awoke from this dream quite disturbed.

A few months later, my mother asked me if I remembered a boy named Gary that I used to play with. Then she shared some bad news: Gary had recently died of leukemia. I immediately recalled my dream and knew almost certainly that I had dreamed about him the day he died, or close to that time. I was impressed by this seemingly telepathic or possibly precognitive dream. A few years later, when my mother took a parapsychology course at the university and talked about ESP (extra sensory perception) and the paranormal powers of the mind, my curiosity accelerated.

Although I attended church until I left for college, I had started doubting the truth of the Bible, and around age seventeen made a conscious decision to reject Christianity and explore other religions.

One night while in college, as I was driving with friends down an unfamiliar dirt road, I suddenly had a fear that I might hit a dog and immediately slowed down. "Wouldn't it be awful if I hit a dog?" I asked my friends. They seemed surprised at this random comment and shrugged it away. Within a minute, the car's headlights captured three dogs running onto the road. Since I had slowed down, I was able to stop in time. "See," I said to my friends, "it's a good thing I had that premonition!" They were suitably awed.

Fueled by books and further experiences that seemed to have a supernatural source, my interest accelerated after graduation. The study of Eastern religions further augmented awareness of paranormal powers. I was introduced via a guided visualization in a New Age course to my "spiritual master," a spirit guide. I didn't know it at the time, but the meditation techniques and the guided visualizations were actually forms of self-induced hypnosis that put me into an altered state of consciousness.

As I practiced my meditation and the other exercises, my paranormal experiences—including out-of-body experiences—grew. When I finally studied and practiced astrology, becoming a professional, licensed astrologer in 1983 after taking a required seven-hour exam, I was already familiar with feeling supernatural "energy" flowing in me and around me, and from the people around me.

When I looked at trees or stars, I did not see just trees and stars, but levels of reality that contained the presences of wise spiritual beings. If one was advanced enough in the spiritual path, one had access to the guidance offered by these beings. I felt surrounded by benevolent spiritual guides who, I believed, protected me. I plunged into my astrology practice, confident that I was helping others by illuminating the astrological blueprint for their souls and lives. It didn't hurt that I was born on Samhain, an important date in the Pagan calendar. You know this day better as Halloween. And it was on this same day that my son arrived, well before his due date!

I continued to meditate, see, and feel entities in my room (usually in scary ways), and practice astrology. I rationalized the frightening experiences by telling myself that I was being tested or was not yet pure enough to have the exhilarating spiritual experiences. My hatred of Christianity grew. I thought Christians were on a lower level of spiritual growth and understanding.

So it was a shock to me in the spring of 1990, as I was finishing up my term as president of the astrological society, that I felt a strong compulsion to go to church. I did not understand this feeling and resisted it for several months. Finally, on Labor Day weekend, I attended a church and I felt love from a personal God pouring down on me.

This church was surprisingly open-minded and some people even asked for my business card! Thinking I might get more clients, I kept attending. I felt comfortable there, but I began to receive an impression that God didn't like astrology—and then that he wanted me to *give up* astrology.

This impression was so powerful that I did give up astrology—something I had really loved. Against all odds, I started reading the Bible. As I was reading a passage in Matthew 8 shortly before Christmas, my eyes were opened and I understood who Jesus really was. I realized I had been on a path leading away from God my whole life. I turned my life over to Christ and became his. A few months later, I discovered that a young Christian man in an office where I worked part-time and his fellowship group had been praying for me all during 1990!

Since 1990, access to esoteric New Age and occult teachings has grown dramatically; occult concepts are incorporated into entertainment and often promoted in the culture. And these ideas are reaching children at younger and younger ages.

Today's games, television shows, movies, video games, and card games freely and frequently feature ghosts, witches, sorcery, spells, and more, making my past exposure and experiences seem mild by comparison. It's not uncommon for the young hero of a book or television program to be a witch, psychic, or ghost, or to possess psychic or other paranormal abilities. As such things grow more common, cultural desensitization grows. And as the culture is desensitized, we face the following consequences:

1. Our culture accepts the paranormal as harmless, useful, or even good.
2. The paranormal becomes more accessible and appealing to children and teens.
3. Parents become less guarded about the paranormal.
4. Children become less immune to the temptation to explore the paranormal.

What can a parent do?

Step one: Become informed. This book will help you with that. And here's the first thing to learn: The paranormal is essentially the occult arts disguised as fun, as natural abilities, or worse, as advanced wisdom. Fantasy is often in the mix, creating the illusion that the occult is merely imaginary.

Misinformation about the paranormal and the occult abounds. Some material is confusing and inaccurate or sensational; some material downplays the paranormal as harmless fun or as mere fraudulent deception. And while there have always been scam artists who claim psychic abilities, our world today includes many psychics, astrologers, card readers, and mediums who believe in what they do. And what they do isn't mere harmless fun. Many are supported by spiritual strongholds, which, like an iceberg, lie deep beneath the surface.

Having the facts is the first link in the chain of productive proaction. Looking at the data carefully will probably cause concern, but you can (and should) be concerned without being fearful. When parents prayerfully exercise wisdom and discernment, they can tackle these issues with confidence.

I have written this book to inform parents about the basics of the paranormal—the areas of danger, where it exists in our culture, how to identify it—and to offer suggestions for informing and equipping children and teens.

What you read in this book may seem unreal to you. Perhaps, like some Christians, you find it difficult to believe anyone would seriously practice the occult today. Or maybe you assume that those who *are* involved in the occult must be unbalanced people. It would seem to make sense since some occult practices are bizarre. Here's the plain truth: Many *highly intelligent* people are attracted to the occult and become involved in it. In fact, the complexity of some occult teachings is the very thing that attracts many young people.

There is no way to identify every aspect of the occult. Therefore, this book will focus on the basics of the occult and activities that are widely practiced so you can recognize them. There will be no attempt to be sensational; the subject matter itself is sensational enough.

The world of the paranormal is characterized by a wide disagreement on terms, definitions, concepts, and practices. No standard or central authority exists for most of these beliefs and practices. I have attempted to give the most commonly held views while not ruling out the possibility of other opinions. Although the occult is marked by adaptation and diversity, it is certainly possible to grasp the basics so that you are sufficiently informed and equipped for response.

Precisely because of the diversity in the occult, the spellings of terms may vary from group to group. Similarly, whether something is capitalized or not might vary among those in the occult or New Age. In this book, lowercase letters will be used for the following words unless they are referring to a specific group, being, or practice: gnostic, divine, pagan, and witchcraft. In the case of witchcraft, the lowercase indicates the generic practice of witchcraft, which includes various occult practices around the world, as explained in chapter 9. When the modern religion of Witchcraft (also referred to by some as Wicca) is indicated, Witchcraft will be capitalized.

PART ONE:

WHAT IS THE PARANORMAL, AND WHY IS IT A THREAT TO OUR KIDS?

1

WHAT IS THE PARANORMAL? THE HIDDEN AND FORBIDDEN

*W*hen you hear the word *paranormal,* what do you think of? Superman leaping tall buildings? Time machines? Palm reading? Or maybe that TV psychic who says she can see dead people? Bingo on the last two! The first two we'll shelve under the fantasy label and cover later.

Here's a concise definition: The paranormal involves efforts to access or use supernatural power or attempts to gain secret or hidden information outside the use of the natural senses. These practices are otherwise known as the *occult.* Think of ghosts, hauntings, psychics, telling the future, astrology, summoning spirits, sorcery, and incantations. Now you are getting an idea of what the paranormal is about.

It might help to make a distinction between the words *occult* and *cult. Cult* describes an authoritarian organization, usually religious, that strictly monitors and controls the beliefs and activities of its members through fear, threats, and manipulation, whether subtle or overt. Though they may contain many beliefs not unfamiliar to Christians, cults by their very definition deny the essentials of Christian doctrine. *Occult* is a term for sets of practices related to contacting spirits or false gods, seeking supernatural power, and claiming ways to uncover hidden or secret knowledge. These practices are aligned with unique belief systems and can be found in many forms. A cult can have occult practices, but the two terms are not the same.

Paranormal means going above or beyond the normal. *Supernatural* means going beyond the natural. Paranormal and supernatural activities involve the attempted use of invisible forces, energies, powers, or spirits that cannot be objectively discerned or quantified. Keep in mind the key terms: unseen, hidden, and forbidden.

THE MARKS OF THE OCCULT

The occult is not a belief system, but rather an umbrella term for a set of practices that arises from assorted belief systems involving a blend of secret teachings, hidden meanings, and supernatural or paranormal activities.

Some of the marks of the occult include

- attempts to contact or use unseen power or forces not known in the natural world;

- secret or hidden knowledge available only to the initiated;

- secret or hidden information unavailable through natural methods but revealed via supernatural abilities;
- seeing hidden meaning in objects or images;
- practices forbidden by God.

A person can engage in an occult practice independently of a belief that supports it. Anyone can be involved in an occult technique, knowingly or not. There are no "casual observers" at a séance, nor any players who are merely "enjoying a game" when playing with a Ouija board.

The occult includes a range of experiences, from esoteric practices with complex layers of teachings to simplified instructions in a spell book or a deck of tarot cards you can buy at your neighborhood bookstore. Many games marketed today to children include occult references and content too.

Since the occult does not come from one source or religion, elements of it are sometimes mixed in with teachings or beliefs that have a basis in truth, or that even sound Christian. Occult teachings often borrow from the Bible and attempt to counterfeit Christianity. (One such teaching advises followers to say something three times to replicate the Trinity.) Two of the main hallmarks of the occult are that it is based on reading hidden meanings in ordinary patterns, and that it promotes a belief in contacting, accessing, or manipulating unseen things or beings (often described as energy, forces, gods, spirits, or ghosts). Either these unseen beings have no basis in the objective world, or they may be spirit beings (angels).

GOING TO DEUTERONOMY 18

Take a look at Deuteronomy 18:10–14. Here God lists the practices of the occult:

> There shall not be found among you anyone who
> burns his son or his daughter as an offering, anyone
> who practices divination or tells fortunes or interprets
> omens, or a sorcerer or a charmer or a medium or a
> wizard or a necromancer, for whoever does these
> things is an abomination to the LORD. And because of
> these abominations the LORD your God is driving
> them out before you. You shall be blameless before
> the LORD your God, for these nations, which you are
> about to dispossess, listen to fortune-tellers and to
> diviners. But as for you, the LORD your God has not
> allowed you to do this. (ESV)

The Hebrew words translated as "sorcerer," "charmer," or "wizard" here may be different in other Bible translations since Hebrew words often describe actions rather than provide labels, as we find with English words. For example, some versions will use "soothsayer" instead of "observer of times," or will say "one who casts a spell" or "enchanter" instead of "charmer."

Here's the same passage in a different translation.

> There shall not be found among you anyone who
> makes his son or his daughter pass through the
> fire, one who uses divination, one who practices
> witchcraft, or one who interprets omens, or a sor-
> cerer, or one who casts a spell, or a medium, or a
> spiritist, or one who calls up the dead. For whoever
> does these things is detestable to the LORD; and
> because of these detestable things the LORD your

God will drive them out before you. You shall be blameless before the LORD your God. For those nations, which you shall dispossess, listen to those who practice witchcraft and to diviners, but as for you, the LORD your God has not allowed you to do so.

An Old Testament Hebrew word, *qesem*, rendered in this passage as "divination," is sometimes translated as "witchcraft." The biblical prophets Isaiah, Jeremiah, Ezekiel, Micah, and Zechariah mention this practice in a deprecating manner.[1] In addition, there are several Old Testament words from which one can derive the words for sorcerer, witch, astrologer, or magician. Another word in this passage, translated as "witchcraft," is *anan*, and refers to observing times; the practice of soothsaying, spiritism, augury, or witchcraft; or it could mean sorceress, diviner, or fortune-teller.[2]

Hebrew terms for these practices are very descriptive. For example, a word translated as "astrologer" might come from a word meaning to divide up the heavens.[3] In the Old Testament some words translated as "witch" come from the word *kashaph*, meaning to whisper or hiss, so the noun form, *kashshaph*, means an enchanter, sorcerer, or magician. This word is meant to sound like the hiss or whisper of someone doing spells.[4]

WHAT IS DEUTERONOMY 18 TELLING US?

God's view of these practices is clear: They are an abomination. It is significant that God groups the practice of sacrificing children along with the occult practices because it emphasizes just how detestable these acts are and points out that they all stem from turning to false gods.

Despite the range of terms in different Bible versions, it is plain what is being forbidden. Following the order of the text, these practices can be broken down into these categories:

1. Divination or fortune-telling
2. Sorcery, including casting spells
3. Contacting disembodied spirits, including the dead

To dabble or engage in these practices is, first of all, disobedience to God. Secondly, it can lead to contact with the demonic.

Okay, now you have the basics. There's much more to learn in chapter 2.

BRINGING IT HOME

Here are some ways you and your child can go over the Deuteronomy 18 passage:

*   Ask your child to read this passage with you.
*   Ask your child to list in his or her words what this passage is saying about activities God does not like.
*   Make a list of what is mentioned in the passage and work together to divide it into the three categories of divination, sorcery, and spirit contact. Some items might belong in more than one category. (Chapter 2 will go over this in more detail.)

2

HIDDEN MEANINGS, HIDDEN POWERS, HIDDEN BEINGS

[B]y practicing magic you put you [sic] self in a spot where danger and chaos can get to you easier, but if you're willing to learn God will (or nowadays, books and group leaders) teach you how to protect yourself from those negative energies, so you can safely continue on a magical path (which for some people is a better path than maybe Christianity, or Buddhism, etc.) to become closer to him (god) and learn his love and secrets like no other man or woman would imagine.[1]

Like I said before I've been in to Magick and the Occult sents [sic] I was 10 years old. When I was 15 years old I become a member of an Occult Order here in C____ ...
Do you know about the Temple of Set? I am planning to become [sic] a member of it so I can study the most advance [sic] forms of Black Magick.[2]

29

*B*reak out a magnifying glass and closely examine the three terms: divination, sorcery, and spirit contact. Note that these three areas involve the paranormal and sometimes overlap with each other. Now grab a nice cup of coffee or tea and get comfortable for this tour through the terms of the hidden and forbidden.

BREAKING DOWN THE TERMS

1. Divination: Hidden Meanings

Divination, often called fortune-telling, is retrieving information by using paranormal methods or by reading hidden meaning where there is no apparent meaning. Divination may require an ability that goes beyond the five senses, such as psychic powers; or it may involve a tool or system that assists in the extraction of hidden meaning from the natural world. One source defines divination as "the effort to gain information of a mundane sort by means conceived of as transcending the mundane."[3]

Psychic powers most commonly include telepathy, which is receiving or sending thoughts to another person; precognition, a knowledge of the future; clairvoyance, the ability to see the past, present, or future; and psychometry, the ability to "read" an object by holding it, thus gaining information about the owner or past owners and history of the object. Psychics may also contact or channel spirits, such as spirit guides or angels, or beings they consider to be from another planet, galaxy, or dimension.

Many forms of divination are familiar: astrology, tarot cards, palmistry, numerology, tea-leaf reading, pendulum, scrying (gazing into an opaque surface), and runes (symbols inscribed on stones or cards). Astrology is based on a belief that the planets and their positions have a meaning related to a person's life. Tarot cards are tools used for reading hidden messages. For most people, the lines on their palms are simply lines, but for palm readers, the hand itself is a tool whose shape and lines contain hidden meaning. Almost anything can be used as a divinatory tool; the actual instrument is not important.

Interpreting omens from nature, something mentioned in the Deuteronomy passage, is a category of divination sometimes called *augury*. An omen is often believed to be a sign of an impending event. Patterns in clouds and smoke or in the way birds were flying were read in ancient times to discern the will of gods. Other omens became part of folk superstitions, such as the idea that dropping a spoon on the floor meant a guest was coming to visit, or breaking a mirror would bring seven years of bad luck. A lot of superstitions as well as the belief in luck reflect an occult way of thinking.

2. Sorcery, Casting Spells, Magic:[4] Hidden Powers

These practices include an attempt to access, channel, or manipulate a power or energy that is not natural or measurable in order to bring about a desired end. Turning on a light switch in order to get electricity is not sorcery! Electricity has known components that can be identified and measured; there is objective, consistent data about it. When dealing with paranormal energy or forces, however, there is no known data or objective, verifiable components.

Those who practice magic mainly include three groups: those from indigenous cultures who practice shamanism and are considered to be the mediators between the spirit world or gods and the people of the community; magicians who use a complex system of ritual or ceremonial magic; and Wiccans or Witches, followers of an earth-based religion who believe that the earth and nature are sacred and are often polytheistic.

At the core of nature magic is a belief in the elements of air, earth, water, and fire, and belief in the *elementals*, which are the spirits of the elements. These elementals can take animal or human form. Such spirits appear in many folktales around the world under different names (sometimes equated with "fairy" or "deva"[5]) and are typically considered mischievous, deceptive, and even dangerous to humans. Elementals are summoned, or conjured, in magical rituals to be used by the magician or witch, and then dispatched. Water elementals are known as Nymphs or Undines; the earth elementals are Gnomes; the air spirits are Sylphs; and the fire elementals are Salamanders. Because these spirits are linked to the elements of nature, they are considered "natural" and not supernatural, especially by Wiccans and Witches.

In some magical systems, the elementals are ruled by "higher beings," called Lords of the Watchtowers who, in turn, are ruled by the Mighty Ones, the Old Ones, or the Guardians. Sometimes the Lords of the Watchtowers are equated with the Guardians, depending on the magical system being used. When some Wiccans or Witches cast a circle, they call the corners, which can be considered to be the Elementals, Guardians, or Watchtowers, and even other terms are used.

Sorcery is a word not commonly used today by those in the occult, as it implies the use of black magic (magic to do harm). In the past, it also carried a negative connotation, though its meaning varies in different cultures.

Shaman is a term associated with the practice of magic and the paranormal that has become popular today through the New Age movement. Shamanism emphasizes trance and ecstatic states, often induced through hallucinogenic plants or drugs, spirit contact, contact with or talking to animal spirits, leaving the body, and healing.[6] These practices are drawn from several cultures: Native American, various Latin American indigenous groups, Hawaiian, Eskimoan, and others. Traditionally, the shaman is the community's healer and link to the spirit world, and is looked to as the local wise man or woman. The word *shaman*, however, has been Westernized and has taken on additional or new meanings, so that the definition is no longer clear or agreed upon. Nevertheless, it is being used today, usually in concert with the use of paranormal powers.

All of the above involve the use of one or more of the following: rituals, magical tools, visualization, incantations,[7] magical potions, drugs, or other objects or methods whereby one is seeking to bring about a desired end. These practices often include contact with spirits, whether these spirits are believed to be angels, gods, or other disembodied entities. Visualization is a method for picturing a desired goal clearly in the mind and believing it is already accomplished in order to bring it into reality. This often is part of a technique to bring one into altered states of consciousness.

Ceremonial magic can involve complex rituals and spirit contact. Spells done by Wiccans or Witches often involve casting a circle, incantations, visualization, and invoking gods or goddesses. Techniques such as candle magic involve burning a certain color of candle, often along with visualization or incantations. Such practices vary, however, and there is no standard procedure.

White magic is generally considered harmless and benevolent because it is done for a good purpose, while black magic is done to gain power over someone or to harm. Not everyone in the occult agrees on these distinctions or definitions, and often the line between the two blurs. God's Word, however, is unmistakable that *any* such activity, whether considered benevolent or harmful, is strongly condemned.

3. Spiritism: Hidden Beings

An attempt to contact a disembodied spirit or entity is spiritism, and an attempt to contact the dead is called necromancy in the Bible. Necromancy was performed to get information about the future from the dead. This is what King Saul did when he consulted the medium (or "witch" in some translations) of Endor and asked her to call up the spirit of Samuel (see 1 Samuel 28:7). Mediums today are psychics who specialize in contacting the dead.

Contacting spirits is often done to gather information, and so it can be a form of divination. Many people in the New Age and the occult have spirit guides, who are supposedly benevolent and wise spiritual counselors. For some, these spirit guides are believed to be angels; others consider them to be advanced spiritual masters who have previously lived on Earth but have ascended to higher realms; and in some cases they are believed to be aliens.

The spirits of the Bible are not dead people or special guides; they are angels: either heavenly angels serving God, or fallen angels serving Satan, also known as demons. God forbids contacting spirits, and this includes angels, good or bad.

JOSEPH'S CUP, URIM AND THUMMIM, AND CASTING LOTS

References to divination in the Bible might raise a few questions, if not an eyebrow or two. Genesis 44:5 refers to a cup of "divination" belonging to Joseph. In verse 15, Joseph himself says, "Do you not know that such a man as I can indeed practice divination?" Joseph lived in a culture where divination was commonly practiced to discern the will of the gods. As a ruler second only to Pharaoh, it is not surprising that Joseph would have had such a cup given to him, but it does not mean he used it. When Joseph asks this question, his brothers are still unaware of who he really is. He is playing the part of an Egyptian ruler, and it is true that one in his position might be expected to do divination.

It is also possible Joseph is referring to his past ability to interpret dreams, an ability that came from God and therefore is not divination. God's Word does not contradict itself, and a narrative about this cup of divination in no way endorses divination, nor does it override God's commandments against such divination. And don't forget that Bible characters chosen and used by God often did things that were wrong.

Let's look next at Urim and Thummim. These are first referred to in Exodus 28 in a passage describing the priests' garments. The Lord gives instruction in verse 30 that "in the breastpiece of judgment you shall put the Urim and the Thummim, and they shall be on Aaron's heart, when he goes in before the LORD. Thus Aaron shall bear the judgment of the people of Israel on his heart before the LORD regularly" (ESV). God does not give the specifics on the Urim and Thummim, but many scholars believe that these were stones carried in the ephod (or apron) of the priest and used to inquire of the Lord. Unger states that the closest translation of these words is "light" and "perfection,"[8] which still does not give us much to go on. In 1 Samuel 14:41, Saul asks God for guidance in a particular sin, asking the Lord to "give

Urim" if the guilt is his and Jonathan's, and to "give Thummim" if the guilt is Israel's (ESV).

Whatever the Urim and Thummim were, they were designed and used according to God's instructions. *God* initiated this method of consulting him; therefore, this is not coming from man and is not divination forbidden by God. It is reasonable to infer that the lack of details about these objects might be a good thing; otherwise, people undoubtedly would try to replicate them in a mistaken attempt to get answers from God.

Casting lots was practiced by pagans. This was done by the pagan sailors aboard the ship carrying Jonah and by the soldiers at the cross who cast lots to divide up the garments of Jesus. However, in Leviticus 16, God directs Aaron to cast lots over two goats to determine which goat will be the sin offering and which one will be sent to the wilderness. In Joshua 18, Joshua casts lots "before the Lord" to divide up territories among certain tribes. In Acts 1, after a season of prayer and consulting Scripture (see verses 14, 20, and 24), the apostles draw lots to determine who would become the twelfth apostle, replacing Judas.

All of these cases of God's people casting lots take place prior to having the indwelling of the Holy Spirit. These accounts are narrative, and doctrine should not come from narrative unless it is supported elsewhere in Scripture. Since casting lots was done either directed by God or before the Holy Spirit was given to believers, it is reasonable to conclude this is not how decisions should be made today. The Bible has no references to casting lots after Acts 1 and no instructions to the early church to make decisions by casting lots.

None of the instances above supports the forbidden practices of divination.

THE ESOTERIC VIEW

People involved in the occult often make a false dichotomy between the linear and rational and the mystical and esoteric (or "hidden"). They believe that to be truly connected to certain powers or spirits, one must let go of reason and rational thinking. They assume that rational thinking limits a person's ability to delve into the deeper parts of self, or into the unfathomable and secret meanings of the world. Nothing is as it appears to be to the occult mind, and all wisdom and truth are hidden. One practitioner of magic, a Neopagan, put it this way, "It has everything to do with the fundamental reality that the religious experience is highly personal. You can't describe it to anyone in words ... there are no words ... you can only experience these things by 'revelation'— direct revelation thru the divine."[9]

In my studies of and involvement in psychic development and Eastern beliefs, I discovered that nonlinear thinking was highly valued, and that logic and reason were disparaged as too "Western." The idea here was that logical thinking had obscured and suppressed the true, deeper spirituality that could only emerge when the mind was bypassed or tuned out. The goal of meditation techniques based on Eastern beliefs is *not* to think. One Zen teaching states that truth is beyond words (but of course, words must be used to say this!).

Every source I encountered taught that a person cannot enter a mystical state, develop psychic powers, or have true spiritual progress through reason. Such a belief supports the idea that truth is whatever you experience. This embrace of the nonrational assumes that truth can only be realized without reason or thought. Yet consider this irony: Reason and logic *must* be used in order to state this view! Statements against reason and logic are self-refuting, because no one can claim that reason obscures truth without using reason in making such a statement.

God told us to love him with heart, soul, and mind—our whole being (see Matthew 22:37; Mark 12:30; Luke 20:27). God has given us his Word in the Bible, and, of course, words are based on reason and logic. Although it's important to avoid pride in intellect or reason, any belief system that belittles thinking should be considered suspect.

ALTERED STATES

Many in the occult purposely attempt to go into altered states to be able to receive or see the desired information better, or to contact spirits. This state is also referred to as "centering," "getting centered," "centering down," or simply "meditating."

In my local library several years ago, I came across a book in the young-adult section (for preteens and teens) that gave advice on fortune-telling techniques. The author emphasized the need for centering as a prelude to practicing any of the techniques. She stated that centering "may become more important than the reading itself."[10] An expert on crystal healing urges the reader to use the crystal to help achieve "an altered state of mind to access information which you otherwise wouldn't know" and that this altered state is also called a "trance state," which can allow one to "'see' the future or past."[11] This view is standard in the occult.

Achieving an altered state is attempted through meditation, visualization, repetitive body movements such as ecstatic dancing, chanting, and/or through certain hallucinogenic drugs. In cultures where shamanism[12] is common, the shamans use plants or potions to get into this state so they can travel out of body or to commune with spirits. It is commonly acknowledged in the New Age and the occult that certain drugs provide similar experiences to this kind of altered state.

The most common Western methods for discovering an altered state are meditation and visualization. These typically involve specific breathing patterns, techniques to let go of thoughts, focusing on an object, and the repetitive use of a word. This kind of meditation has so penetrated our culture that it has been marketed as a relaxation technique. However, even occultists recognize that the true altered state is much more than relaxation. "True Meditation" involves not just the body, but also the mind, says Donald Michael Kraig, author of *The Truth About Psychic Powers.* He goes on to state that relaxation is "only the first stage leading to True Meditation."[13] In the stage of true meditation, "the little voice which is in your head, the voice which is always conscious, is silenced."[14]

People who practice meditation daily can fall into an altered state easily. For some, simply beginning a psychic reading can trigger this state. I practiced Eastern meditation for a number of years prior to becoming an astrologer. Doing an astrology chart reading would usually—and effortlessly—initiate the altered state. Keep in mind that a person in an altered state is receptive to whatever influence may come to the mind. During this time, a person's critical thinking skills and judgment are suspended. This opens up the person to new ways of thinking—ways that can begin to seem "normal" even when they are not.

THROUGH A DARK GLASS

I used to sit on my bed after reading a portion of *Seth Speaks* (a book "channeled" by Jane Roberts) and practice the mental exercises suggested by the character Seth, who was an "oversoul"—a supposedly advanced being in another dimension. His advice always sounded so wise and helpful. Following Seth's instructions, I would close my eyes and envision the room being empty except for myself, then the neighborhood empty, then the city empty, and so forth, until I reached the point where I was the only one in existence. This exercise, along with my Eastern meditations, subtly affected the way I saw things.

In time, I no longer saw reality as "real," but as an illusion that was masking a deeper reality. This deeper reality was not accessible to everyone, only to those willing, like myself, to stretch their minds and spirits beyond the normal way of seeing things. In these small ways, a mind can shift into a new gear, until objective reality becomes a plethora of realities, and truth multiplies into "levels" of truth. And when this happens, the idea of absolute truth becomes a myth.

Are these things real? Or are they just imaginary head-trips? That issue is the topic of the next chapter.

BRINGING IT HOME

Use the following ideas to help your child understand the basics of the paranormal and the occult. Though it may seem a daunting task at first, simply focus on the various terms one at a time and you can cover the ground quickly.

- With your child, write down each category on a separate sheet of paper: divination, sorcery, and spirit contact (or spiritism). Then, under each category, list the phrase that describes it, such as "hidden meaning" for divination.

- Write a brief definition, then work together to come up with several examples for each category. If you have older children, have them help you with the definitions, too.

- Explore the concept of "esoteric" by asking your child how we can know something (like love) even though we can't actually see it, and compare that to an occult (esoteric) teaching about something we can't see (such as the teaching that claims the lines on our hand have a hidden meaning). What are the differences between these two concepts?

- Discuss God's place in each of these teachings and help your child to see that when something is from God, it is good ... and when it is not, it is a dangerous teaching to accept.

3

FANTASY
VS.
THE PARANORMAL

Finally, the Gods and Goddesses I worship
now seem to care a whole heck of a lot more
for me than any generic Christian God ever did.
I am taking a new subject and I am succeeding.
I have gotten surprise money that I never
even knew I had. And I have discovered
new powers I never even knew I had.[1]

*D*id you ever wish you could be Superman? What intrigued you most, the X-ray vision, the super strength, or the ability to fly? One reason Superman remains an icon is that many children wish they could fly. This is a natural urge to want to escape or be free of normal restrictions (like doing homework or washing the dishes). This is the realm of fantasy and imagination.

Many believe that the paranormal and fantasy are one and the same. Fantasy, however, is simply the use of imaginative abilities, something writers and artists employ often as they spin unfamiliar worlds out of mostly familiar objects, places, and creatures. Fantasy itself is not connected to the practices we see in Deuteronomy 18. Superman's feats aren't explicitly forbidden in the Bible.

Children like to play "pretend" and make things up, and they can easily imagine whatever they wish when playing. This trait is God-given, healthy, and normal. Imagination is a part of life, especially for those who are gifted creatively in the arts. Fantasy books can be entertaining as well as stimulating to a child's imagination. God the Creator, who made us in his image, gave us the ability to be creative.

FANTASY PERVERTED

Sometimes fantasy is used to promote the paranormal. This is significant because preteens and teens are attracted to the mystery and apparent power of fantasy, and younger children tend to imitate behavior they see or read about. This brings up a moral question. If magic is presented (through fantasy) as fun or as a way to fight something evil, then children naturally believe that not only is there nothing wrong with it, but it is a good thing. Many parents tell me that their children or children's friends began to pretend casting spells after viewing a movie or reading a book that presented magic in a positive way. Casting spells seemed like a fun thing to do because they were imitating fictional heroes and heroines.

Some books and movies mix fantasy—flying on a broom or entering other time periods—with actual occult activities such as casting spells, using charms, talking to dead people, or using a divinatory tool such as astrology.

One of the characters in the television series *Charmed* (a show about glamorous sisters who are witches) has the ability to freeze time. Another sister can have visions of the future. While freezing time is not condemned in Deuteronomy nor is it traditionally an occult art, having visions of the future is clearly a form of psychic divination. In *Buffy the Vampire Slayer*, Buffy has superhuman strength to fight off incredibly strong adversaries. Her friend Willow, who is studying Wicca, casts spells. While Buffy's powers are purely imaginative, what Willow is doing is forbidden by God. This mixture of fantasy and the occult can lead some to think that all the activities are fantasy, when in fact, some of them are real occult practices.

Blending the two together presents a mixed message to children, especially younger children who are unable to discern what is dangerous or to filter out lies, even when they know instinctively that certain things in the book or movie might not be good or true.

Some people defend books that commend occult powers by saying that readers are old enough to know the difference between reality and fantasy. This may be true for some readers, but the greater issue is not whether a child can tell reality from fantasy, but whether the book or movie gives a positive spin to occult paranormal practices.

When my son was in the fourth grade, his teacher read a book to the class that bothered him. Both of us were new Christians at the time, and I had explained to him why the things of the occult were wrong, but he was too young to articulate why the book was troubling him.

At the public library one day, my son came across the book being read in class and showed it to me by pulling it *partly* from the shelf. He did not bring it to me, possibly because he knew this was a big issue and it might upset me, or because he felt conflicted about "telling" on his teacher, whom he liked. Young children often feel a loyalty to their teachers and friends. Don't miss the implications of this truth: Because of this loyalty, it's important for *parents* to take the initiative and be aware of what children are reading or seeing in school.

When I read the book at the library, I realized why my son was uneasy. The hero of the book was a young man born with "natural" psychic abilities who felt different from those around him. He became the apprentice to a traveling magician with supernormal powers. As the story progressed, the young man came to realize that the magician used his powers for gain and to harm people, setting him up for a showdown with the villain.

The showdown involved the use of the young man's psychic and magical abilities, which were presented clearly as supernatural. Beneath the surface message of the hero's bravery and goodness was another message, whether intentional or not, that one could use psychic or supernatural powers for good, in order to fight evil. This is the philosophy of white magic and white witchcraft. And this is what had caused my son's unease.

IS THE PARANORMAL IMAGINARY OR REAL?

Some people believe that all occult practitioners are frauds. While it is true that there are scam artists among the card readers, psychics, and palmists, there are also genuine followers of occult practices who experience, or believe they experience, something real.

I recall my agnostic father asking me, after I had been a professional astrologer for a few years, if I believed in astrology. This question was insulting to me because it implied I was doing something I didn't believe was valid, which clearly meant that I was either a fraud or a fool. I also have had Christians query me about my former life as an astrologer and ask if I was a "quack" or if I had been conning people. They truly thought I was making things up for my clients.

I told my father that not only did I believe in astrology, but I would not do anything I did not have faith in. He asked why I believed in it, and I fervently replied, "Because it works!" I thought that astrology was my "calling" in this lifetime (I also believed in reincarnation and that I had lived previous lives), and I would not have dedicated myself to something I thought was false. This was true for astrologers I knew, and for the tarot card readers, psychics, palm readers, and others I knew who were involved in these practices.

Some say that the practices in Deuteronomy 18 specifically relate to calling on gods or spirits, and if this is not being done, then one is not really practicing an occult art. Do fallen angels care if someone believes he or she is calling on them? They are more than happy to get involved, and occult practices and tools are designed to initiate such a response.

I never called on my spirit guide when doing astrology, attempting out-of-body travel, exerting a psychic "power," reading tarot cards, or other occult-related practices. I believe the mere engagement in such practices and the use of occult tools can and does engage the demonic, whether or not there is a belief or desire for supernatural contact.

CALLUSES ON THE SOUL

Whether or not there is a real power in the paranormal world of the occult is a debated issue. Some respected Christians believe there is no power in the occult, that it is imagined or made up. Having been involved in these areas for many years before becoming a Christian, I would challenge that view. I believe there *is* a power there, but it is definitely not from God.

Part of the effect of the occult is that it preys on and plays with the mind. Much of the damage from the occult is in this area. So even if you don't believe there is a supernormal power in the occult, please believe that it does have an effect on people. And whether it is psychological or spiritual, or a combination of the two, it is a *negative* effect. Part of the effect is a desensitization to the bizarre, to violence, and to evil. This desensitization gradually increases, but often in ways so subtle, the person is unaware of it. It is as if invisible calluses develop on the person's spirit, mind, and emotions. This effect may only be noticeable to others after a period of time.

The Bible speaks of desensitization in Ephesians: "So I tell you this, and insist on it in the Lord, that you must no longer live as the Gentiles do, in the futility of their thinking. They are darkened in their understanding and separated from the life of God because of the ignorance that is in them due to the hardening of their hearts. Having lost all sensitivity, they have given themselves over to sensuality so as to indulge in every kind of impurity, with a continual lust for more" (Ephesians 4:17–19 NIV).

I experienced this desensitization and the drastic change it made to my worldview and attitudes. I was in bondage to beliefs in reincarnation, the need to meditate daily in order to advance spiritually, the fear of thinking negative thoughts, and other such ideologies. I was also desensitized to the weird and the bizarre. I was not aware of these bondages at the time, but instead, ironically enough, felt a tremendous sense of freedom. Nor was I aware how desensitized I was until after I became a Christian. The Lord freed me and gently began the process of resensitizing the calloused areas of my mind, heart, and soul. It took a few years for me to be aware of this, and I was well into my Christian walk before I fully understood the damaging effects of my previous life.

READING ISN'T ACTUALLY DOING IT, SO WHAT'S THE HARM?

Here's the big question that's probably knocking on your brain right now: Does reading books or watching television shows with occult or paranormal content have the same effect as participating in these activities? And the answer? It probably doesn't have the *same* effect, but it can add to the desensitization. You know the old saying, "Garbage in, garbage out"? I think you will agree that what gets put into the mind affects thinking, feelings, and often behavior. Our society certainly believes this about children; thus, the ratings systems for movies, video games, and music, and kid-safe filters for televisions and computers.

Responsible parents need to do their best to keep their children from being exposed to anything and everything, even if they think their children know the difference between reality and fantasy. And whether a story is true or fictional, it can have an effect on a reader. Words are powerful. They can call up vivid images that are difficult to erase or forget. Human beings are not robots—we react on many levels to what we read, see, and hear.

REAL PEOPLE, REAL EFFECTS

A fifteen-year-old girl sought me out at a youth retreat where I spoke. At first she could not even speak, and I saw fear in her eyes. When I told her that she could tell me anything, she finally admitted that she thought she was losing her mind. She had been practicing Witchcraft and casting spells for about a year and wanted to stop, but whenever she tried to stop casting spells, things in her life fell apart. She was afraid to stop.

This is similar to the story from another teen, who had been wearing a ring with supposed protective powers that had been given to her by the priestess of her Witchcraft coven. This young girl was being drawn to Christ, had started going to church, and had chosen to take off the ring. However, she kept putting it back on because, she told me, bad things happened when she took it off.

In both of these cases it is quite possible nothing supernatural was going on, though it would be difficult to know either way. However, it was clear in each case that the girls' minds had been strongly affected—one was in bondage to casting spells, the other to wearing her "protective" ring. This bondage is a very real result of occult practices.

SPIRITUAL EFFECTS

Whether or not these situations have actual spiritual components may be up for debate, but I believe there is clearly a spiritual foundation beneath such practices. It is clearly best to avoid them if at all possible. Consider Philippians 4:8: "Finally, brothers, whatever is true, whatever is honorable, whatever is just, whatever is pure, whatever is lovely, whatever is commendable, if there is any excellence, if there is anything worthy of praise, think about these things" (ESV). Similarly, we are to clothe ourselves with the Lord Jesus (see Romans 13:14), and fix our eyes on Jesus (Hebrews 12:2).

Good advice, to be sure. Yet the culture is filled with occult and paranormal references and content. Where in the culture are these practices? We'll explore that in the next chapter.

BRINGING IT HOME

How can children understand that the occult is not fantasy when often these two are mixed together? Here are some suggestions.

- Ask your child to describe what imagination is, or to give an example of it.

- If your children have read fairy tales or fantasy stories, ask them what makes those stories just "pretend."

- Show your child the list you made together at the end of chapter 2. Ask him or her if this is imagination or fantasy—or something else. Listen to the answers and clear up confusion.

- Ask your child to tell a short made-up story, and then ask him to tell you a true story of something he saw or experienced. Talk about the differences.

- Assure your child that the imaginary stories are okay as long as they are not presented as factual, and the factual should not be presented as imaginary.

4

BEWITCHING
ENTERTAINMENT

Powerful Places: Some spells need atmosphere—and your bright pink bathroom just won't do. Get outside and work with Mother Nature to make some magick under the sun or the stars, near trees or water. The energy of all living things will add their power to yours. [Advice on casting spells on Scholastic Inc. Web site for kids][1]

After that I read Enochian Magic for Beginners *by Donald Tyson I became very fascinated with the high magical arts then and it made more sense to me than witchcraft.[2]*

WHAT IS THE APPEAL?

Judy, a Christian friend of mine, was in a group of coworkers when one of them started talking about being an astrologer and how many people were helped by her astrology practice. The others, transfixed by this, were keenly interested to know more. Judy wondered why no one was drawn to her, a Christian, the way they were drawn to this astrologer.

The god of this age is Satan, and what he offers is enticing and desirable. A lost world naturally bends in the direction opposed to God. What glitters are those things that feed and ease the sinful nature and reassure humans that they have their own power and their own wisdom. It is appealing in a fallen world to think that we can be naturally good or divine, or can become that way, and therefore do not need judgment.

The possibility of connecting with a supernatural power makes children and teenagers (and adults) feel strong and bold. It reinforces pride. It feeds the desire to be important. The belief that the paranormal might actually work makes it all the more attractive. Well, does it work? Several possibilities suggest why it might *seem* to work, and one reason for why it might actually work.

1. The person may imagine results.

2. Certain results may be from unconscious physical actions by the participant (such as moving the pointer on the Ouija board).

3. Results may have a natural explanation.

4. Results may be coincidental and may have happened anyway. For example, if a girl casts a spell to get a certain boy to ask her out and he does indeed ask her out, she may assume the result is due to the spell. However, this could just be

coincidence. The boy may have asked the girl out anyway.

5. Results may arise from demonic activity.

Several factors explain why children and teens are easily attracted to the paranormal, and why it is particularly dangerous for them. Children are more vulnerable to the paranormal and to things that promote it because they are more inexperienced in the world and more gullible. Additionally, most children under twelve haven't yet developed sufficient critical thinking skills necessary for evaluating the issues and principles involved. It's especially difficult for them when wrong ideas or practices are blended in with right ones.

Some children and teens under strict control of parents are drawn to the paranormal by the promise of having their own power and control. This desire for power and control is normal, but it can become dangerous if they seek this in the paranormal or occult practices. Another factor is a child or teen's keen curiosity—most are intrigued and challenged by the unknown. This curiosity is heightened and exploited by television shows depicting "real" haunted houses, ghosts, aliens, disappearances of objects or people, "unknown" mysterious happenings, and other inexplicable events that pique interest in the paranormal. Although most of these accounts likely have natural explanations or are outright hoaxes, children and teens are fascinated by these tales and tend to believe them. These stories can lead to an unhealthy interest in the paranormal. There is also the taboo factor: Preteens and teens in particular are often attracted to that which is forbidden or thought strange by parents or other adults. Finally, many teenagers (and adults) who are disillusioned by Christianity seek out the paranormal as an alternative that purports to answer the questions that were left unanswered by their Christian faith.

Here's a brief summary of why the paranormal appeals to children and teens:

1. A desire for power and control
2. The lure of the unknown
3. The lure of the forbidden
4. The need to feel special
5. The desire to rebel against parents or the norm
6. The belief that the paranormal gives results
7. Disillusionment with Christianity

TO BE OR NOT TO BE LUCKY: MAGICAL THINKING AND CHARMS

Magical thinking is making a connection between things or events that have no actual cause-and-effect relationship. For example, if a baseball player thinks his team will win the game if he wears his lucky socks, well, that is magical thinking. Everyone knows that a pair of socks cannot make anyone win a game. But the thinking behind a lucky object, which the baseball player is undoubtedly blissfully unaware of, is that a special energy in the object will be imparted to him and to the team to make them win, or that the special object will attract a winning energy.

Magical thinking is pagan thinking. If you were to examine the origins of most superstitions about luck, such as knocking on wood, carrying a rabbit's foot or lucky penny, hanging a horseshoe over the doorway, or others, you would find that these concepts were based on beliefs in appeasing gods, powers, or chance; attracting supernatural powers for protection against evil; or some other superstitious view of attracting good fortune. Luck and so-called lucky objects have nothing to do with relying on God.

Carrying an object for luck is actually using the object as an amulet or a charm. The word *charm* itself originally was associated with magic and spells. To charm someone meant to put a spell on that person. Magic in all cultures includes the belief in objects or charms having special powers. An *amulet* is an object supposedly imbued with magical powers to keep the wearer safe from evil forces or events, and a charm supposedly attracts good fortune to the wearer. Such thinking assumes the particular object carries a power, and thus also is giving honor to the object and source of power.

This kind of thinking is at work in the marketing of necklaces and bracelets inscribed with Chinese symbols for good fortune, good health, love, long life, or prosperity. This is partly the result of a rising interest in Feng Shui, a complex set of divination techniques used to arrange and place objects so that the "universal life energy" will flow more smoothly in a physical location. Feng Shui uses Chinese characters that indicate fortune, prosperity, or happiness at certain locations in the home or office to attract "good energy." Jewelry with these symbols is marketed to the public with the suggestion that wearing these pieces will bring health, happiness, love, or luck. This is similar to wearing an amulet or carrying a lucky charm.

ASTROLOGY, OUIJA BOARDS, SPELLS, AND MORE

The marketplace and the media are full of products and entertainment that not only promote belief in the paranormal but also portray it as a good thing. Products, movies, and television shows come and go, so a focus on specific examples is not always helpful; however, I'll show you a few examples in this chapter so you see how prevalent this is (and discover clues about what to look out for from future marketplace-and-media products).

Let's take a look at some of the marketplace-and-media offerings available at the writing of this book.

Tarot cards are sold in most of the major chain bookstores. Tarot cards come in multiple types, and some are marketed as meditation images but are, in effect, also designed for divination. Other types include Witchcraft tarot decks, vampire decks, the Thoth deck (designed by ceremonial magician Aleister Crowley), Native American decks, Celtic decks, Goddess decks, Egyptian-themed decks, and numerous others.

Print media entertainment includes horoscopes in magazines (especially magazines for girls and women) and newspapers. Electronic media includes TV shows that offer a "lighthearted" take on Witchcraft such as *Sabrina, the Teenage Witch*, a glamorous view as in *Charmed*, or feature a "good" character who practices Witchcraft such as in *Buffy the Vampire Slayer* (Buffy's best friend, Willow, was the Wiccan); cartoons with characters who use crystals, spells, or spirit contact, such as *Scooby-Doo* cartoons; and an endless stream of movies for children that have subtle or blatant promotion of paranormal activities (the most popular of which is the Harry Potter series, based on the books by J. K. Rowling). *Charmed* actually incorporates the *Book of Shadows*, a compilation of rituals and spells actually used by those who practice Witchcraft, in some episodes. Horoscope columns in newspapers are usually placed near the comics, ensuring that a lot of young people will see them.

Nonfiction books marketed to children, preteens, and teens teach Wicca, how to cast spells, do magic (sorcery),

learn fortune-telling, contact spirits, develop psychic powers, and other paranormal practices. The 1996 movie *The
Craft* was credited by witches themselves with getting a lot
of teens interested in modern Witchcraft. A statement in a
pro-Witchcraft magazine noted that: "Whether you loved it
or hated it, *The Craft* created a surge of interest in magick,
the occult, and Witchcraft."[3] A young man who practices
Witchcraft told an interviewer that he first got involved at
age eleven and did his first ritual based on what he had seen
in *The Craft*.[4]

The book *Teen Witch*[5] was released in 1998 and sold so
many copies that it went through numerous printings in a
very short time. This is a nonfiction book that gives advice
on how to do Witchcraft. A spell kit was created to go along
with it and also sold well. Several teens have told me they
first got into Wicca after reading this book. The same
author has written several other books, including *Angels,
Companions in Magick*,[6] in which the author gives specific
instructions on summoning spirits.

In the Harry Potter series, the hero and his friends
spend most of their time in a school where they take courses
on how to cast spells, do astrology and other forms of divination, and make potions to be used in spells. The Potter
books and movies refer to amulets and charms, dead people
who have become ghosts, black magic such as the spell cast
by the villain in order to give himself a body, psychic powers that are innate in Harry through his scar, and
communication with the dead (Harry's parents).

The popularity of Harry Potter inspired an onslaught of
new books for teens and preteens with paranormal themes
and characters, including the *Sweep* series by Cate Tiernan,
Circle of Three by Isobel Bird, *Daughters of the Moon* by
Lynne Ewing, and *T*witches*, published by Scholastic Inc.[7]

According to a story in the *Pittsburgh Post-Gazette*,
"Scholastic publisher and editor in chief Jean Feiwel said

the new series have merely tapped into an increased teen interest in witches. 'It's almost gotten—dare I say it—acceptable,' Feiwel said. There's no doubt that fantasy and wizards have become more popular because of Harry Potter. Practicing witches are amused by this trend in teen books. 'It's nice to see that we are not always the bad guys anymore,' laughed Wren Walker, cofounder of 'The Witches Voice,' an umbrella Web site for Witchcraft groups."[8]

An article on *Publishers Weekly Online* exploring the popularity of pagan books among younger readers noted that *Teen Witch* had sold more than fifty thousand copies. Llewellyn's director of trade sales stated that his company (which publishes occult titles) started "repackaging 'classic' pagan titles with more youthful covers, and sales often jumped tenfold as a result."[9] In 2003, *Publishers Weekly* featured another article on the increasing popularity of New Age and occult books, including the growing market for these titles for preteens and teens.[10]

Children like to imitate what they read about. A third-grade teacher noted, "If you get a whole group of kids together who read Harry Potter, it becomes a little club, and they want to dress, talk, and act just like the characters in the book."[11] This includes casting spells. A friend of mine told me that her third-grader saw children on the playground at school pretending to cast spells. If occult arts seem to be a game or are taken lightly, children may fail to see the occult as a threat.

And then there is the Internet. Thousands of Web sites promote paranormal techniques and beliefs. Some sites for young children offer fantasies or games that, while not actually being part of occult practices, include occult terms or concepts. The Disney W.I.T.C.H. site, based on a book series, features characters who are "guardians of the veil" and who "harness the power of the elements."[12] At the site, kids can choose "W.I.T.C.H. power practice" or take a quiz to see which guardian they are most like.

Some Web sites owned by companies that market to children are not even related to the occult, but they still may offer occult fare. Scholastic, the U.S. publisher of the Harry Potter series, has a Web site specifically for its young readers. Any child searching for information on its series about teen witches, *T*Witches*, will come across a page giving helpful tips on casting spells.[13] Another page invites kids to send in spells, which are then listed on the Web site "Spellbook."[14]

SO WHERE DOES THIS LEAVE US?

I wrote my first handout on Wicca in 1995 because of a question asked by an eighth-grade boy. He said that a boy in his school who was a Wiccan had told him that the Trinity was a copy of the Wiccan Triple Goddess (maid, mother, and crone). He did not know how to respond to this and wanted my advice. At that point, I did not know the prevalence of Wiccans in the school system. I have since learned about the existence of the vampire subculture in school as well.

Teens don't always ask or tell their parents, Sunday school teachers, or youth leaders about these things. It is up to you the parents (or youth leaders and teachers in the church) to ask questions and try to find out what is going on in your child's school.

You might want to know that there is a dangerous philosophy hidden behind some of these practices. Have you heard of the "dark side"? Ever wonder what it really means? You are about to find out in the next chapter.

BRINGING IT HOME

Use these ideas to find out what your child is being exposed to at school and among peers, and to get him or her thinking about these things.

- Ask your child if he or she ever reads the horoscope, if her school has Wiccans or witches, or if she has played the Ouija board. Don't freak out if you hear "yes" to any of these. Instead, open a discussion by asking your child what she thinks of these things and if they are good or bad.

- Ask your child to list movies or TV shows he has seen that depict good people with paranormal powers. Then ask: Why did these characters need these powers? Could they have been heroes without the powers? Why or why not?

- Ask your child to describe or make a list of what makes a hero or heroine. Which should count the most, good character traits or supernormal powers? Explain.

- Talk to your child about luck—what is it? Is it real? Can an object really bring luck? Talk about how "luck" does or doesn't fit in with a view that God is ultimately in control of everything.

5

THE DARK SIDE

I believe in positive and negative forces. Yes these forces
can appear as absolute good and absolute evil ...
in the spirit world there is only positive and
negative energies and order and chaos.[1]

$\mathcal{I}$n a book about a young wizard by a popular writer of
young-adult literature, a teacher tells a student at a wizardry
school that practicing the black arts is not really evil at all,
merely the exaggeration and twisting of normal human
traits. The teacher says, "By 'black,' I do not mean evil. Or
wicked. I mean dark and deep, as in the black water of the
deepest lakes."[2]

So dark is not evil? The "dark side" is often presented as
a necessary counterpart of the good, or "light" side.

THE YIN AND YANG OF GOOD AND EVIL

The worldviews behind the occult are iffy on good and evil. Many deny the existence of absolute good or evil. Sometimes the terms *light side* and *dark side* or *positive* and *negative* are used as substitutes for *good* and *evil*. If there is a light side and dark side to something, it means that the "something" is common to both the light and dark; that is, the source for both good and evil is the same. This view in the occult is often called polarity.

The best way to understand this is through the symbol for yin and yang, a symbol commonly seen today on jewelry, T-shirts, surfboards, alternative-healing centers, and elsewhere. It is depicted as a circle divided into black and white, with a white dot on the black side and a black dot on the white side. This symbol and the philosophy behind it became associated with Taoism, an ancient Chinese religion with a complex history that arose from early Chinese shamanism and belief in a universal life force called *chi*.

Many people believe that yin and yang represent good and evil, a belief in itself disturbing because the implication is that there is a little evil in good and a little good in evil, represented by the white dot on the black side and vice versa. This is the most common answer I've gotten when asking teenagers what the symbol means to them. Other answers are that it represents peace, harmony, or balance.

In Taoism, the Tao, loosely translated as "the Way" or "the Path," is the origin of all things and the ultimate reality. As is true in many Eastern religions, this concept is said to be beyond one's intellectual grasp since it describes a reality beyond the thinking mind. One book states that those who live according to the Tao have an understanding so profound that they themselves cannot be understood.[3] Therefore, according to Taoist teachings, the truth of the Tao can only be understood indirectly or through a process of enlightened living. Happiness is gained by living in the flow of the Tao, which is the flow of the universe. This belief has no personal God. Where do the yin and yang come in? "Through the dynamics of yin and yang, the female and male cosmic principles, the Tao creates all phenomena. Whereas the Tao is perfectly harmonious, the cosmos is in a state of constant disequilibrium."[4]

Taoism teaches that all is one, but the universe is seemingly divided into two opposing but equal and fluctuating forces. Yang, represented by the white in the yin-yang symbol, stands for the creative, active principle, while yin, represented by black, is dissolution and return (to creation). Yang signifies hot, dry, male, light, hardness, movement, and initiative. Yin symbolizes coolness, moistness, female, darkness, softness, stillness, and receptivity.

The yin and yang forces are believed to be cyclical, moving and evolving into each other, represented by the white dot on the black yin side of the symbol and by the black dot on the white yang side. Taoist teaching suggests that the way to be content is to balance between these two forces.

There is really no good or bad according to the Taoist and yin-yang view, only what *appears* to be good or bad. There is no life and death because "life and death are one, right and wrong are the same."[5]

In this view, opposites are not really opposite; they just appear that way because man supposedly perceives reality through a dualistic conditioning and is unable to see how opposites are really part of the whole. The universe is seen as mystically connected and interplaying through the yin-yang interaction. Referring to the Tao, Chinese sage Wen-Tzu states that "the Way has no front or back, no left or right: all things are mysteriously the same, with no right and no wrong."[6] This view is closely associated with the polarity views in the occult, and in fact, some occult books use the yin-yang symbol to represent views on good and evil. Witches Janet and Stewart Farrar claim that the "Theory of Polarity maintains that all activity, all manifestation, arises from (and is inconceivable without) the interaction of pairs and complementary opposites ... and that this polarity is not a conflict between 'good' and 'evil,' but a creative tension like that between the positive and negative terminals of an electric battery. Good and evil only arise with the constructive or destructive *application* of the polarity's output."[7]

One self-described occultist e-mailed me her view of God and good and evil:

> But I do think we are naturally divine. And I think defining divinity requires that we outgrow our definitions of what morality is, because I think at the end of the day ... God ... whatever god is, doesn't see things in terms of good/bad ... god is energy. God is electricity.... God is some very obscure consciousness that in quantum theory unifies us all at a subatomic level ... It doesn't make distinctions ... only humans do. Morality and distinctions are a product of imperfection.... Judgment is a product of imperfection. It is something we must do in order to navigate our lives by.[8]

The Pagan author of *Out of the Shadows: An Exploration of Dark Paganism and Magick* states: "This polarity of light/dark in Pagan thought is no longer the same as the dualism of good/evil, but rather associated with such complementing principles as creative/destructive, external/internal, attracting/repelling, clarity/mystery, active/passive, solid/flowing, static/dynamic, masculine/feminine, and order/chaos, to name a few."[9]

In the teachings of the Kabbalah, an esoteric belief system based on commentaries on the hidden meanings of the

Torah (the books of Genesis, Exodus, Leviticus, Numbers, and Deuteronomy), evil is considered to be part of good. One Kabbalah expert quotes a story told by a rabbi in which a boy named Israel has the chance to destroy Satan's "heart of evil," which Satan has placed inside a monster, but is unable to do so when he sees the heart bleed, for Israel realizes that "even the heart of evil has within it a spark of the Divine."[10] The lesson, according to the storyteller, is that "even the heart of Satan has a divine spark; even the heart of evil yearns to be redeemed ... our job is not to set up a battleground to eradicate evil, but to search out its spark of holiness."[11] The author quotes the *Zohar*, the sacred book of the Kabbalah, as saying, "There is no sphere of the Other Side (evil) that entirely lacks some streak of light from the side of holiness."[12]

The following concepts are usually found as part of polarity:

1. The source for all opposites is the same, and there are only apparent opposites.

2. The basis for polarity is not good versus evil, but rather that good and evil are part of the complementary opposites of all kinds.

3. Every force needs its opposite to exist.

4. Evil is seen as a force in its own right.

5. Opposite forces sometimes merge with each other and become each other.

6. The goal is balance, so in the ideal situation, all opposites, including good and evil, exist in equal amounts to each other.

A related view is that all opposites, including good and evil, are eventually joined in the one power where distinctions do not matter, but perceiving this comes only with advanced spiritual insight. This view is held by popular New Age writer Deepak Chopra who wrote that in the final stage of knowing God, one realizes that good and evil are swallowed up in God: "What is the nature of good and evil? God is the union of all opposites. Evil no longer exists."[13]

WHITE MAGIC, BLACK MAGIC

In most occult views, there is one source, usually Power or Energy. This is a neutral or amoral force. What determines good or bad is how one *uses* the Power. In the simplest of terms: Good intentions are white magic, and bad intentions are black magic.

It is common to hear or read that modern Witchcraft is all about using magic or spells only for good. The 1996 movie *The Craft*, about four teen witches in a Roman Catholic high school, featured a showdown at the end between one girl, who realized she wanted to use her powers for only good, against the other three. The message of the movie was clear: Practicing white magic or white witchcraft is a good thing.

Some hold the view that even black magic is not always wrong and that the differences between white and black magic are irrelevant. Arthur Edward Waite in his book on ceremonial magic discusses black magic, stating several times that the differences between white and black magic are surface and verbal. In the preface, Waite discusses "the good and evil side of the arts," stating "the two aspects dissolve into one another and belong one to another in the root that is common to both."[14]

A popular creed in Wicca and Witchcraft is "Do no harm, do what you will." But since there is no absolute good or evil, there is no standard by which harm can be judged. Judgments on what is good or evil or "harm" are purely subjective.

LIGHT SIDE, DARK SIDE

Harry Potter and his nemesis, Lord Voldemort, fight using the same power. There is no suggestion that their sources of magic or power are different. In fact, Lord Voldemort once was on the "good" side but fell into the dark side through his own character flaws. Many ties between Harry and the villain reflect the polarity view that good and evil are coupled: Harry's scar gives him a psychic connection to Lord Voldemort, which allows him to sense Voldemort and sometimes enables him to see what the villain is doing through Voldemort's point of view; Harry and Lord Voldemort both speak parselmouth, the language of snakes; they both use a wand that contains part of a feather from the same bird; and in the fourth book, Harry's blood is taken and used to help embody Lord Voldemort, so Lord Voldemort thereafter has some of Harry's blood.

In *Star Wars*, the Force also reflects polarity views of good and evil, as well as the goal to balance these two opposing sides. In *Episode I*, it is suggested that Anakin, the young Darth Vader and future villain, be taken on as a Jedi apprentice despite misgivings about flaws in his character. This is done in order "to balance the Force." In *Episode III: Revenge of the Sith*, Obi-Wan says, "Isn't Anakin the Chosen One? Is he not the one who will bring balance to the Force?"

Even the dark side has its lure. In *Revenge of the Sith*, Anakin is told by the Chancellor, a Sith, that the Jedi and the Sith are similar, except that the Jedi use the light side of the Force while the Sith use the dark side. The Chancellor tells Anakin that the Sith are more advanced in their use of the Force, and are therefore more powerful. His appeal to Anakin to join the dark side succeeds, partly because Anakin believes he can use the Force to save his wife from a future death, and partly because of the lure of power.

This scene with the Chancellor reminded me of a time when I gave a talk at a Christian school. One thirteen-year-old girl waited a long time to speak to me afterwards. She told me she had begun calling on Satan. I said, "How did that make you feel?" She paused, and then said, "Stronger." This view was echoed by someone who found satanism as a teen and told me, "Satanism gives me the strength to be myself despite everyone else's view of things."[15]

Sometimes what is evil is presented simply as strength, or deeper levels of complexity, or even keener intelligence.

The fact that the Force is similar to Taoism is not accidental; filmmaker George Lucas embraced Eastern religions to some extent in his life, even calling himself at one point a "Buddhist Methodist."[16]

THE MORAL FALLOUT

Without a standard for good or evil, right or wrong, there is no moral center. If the source of all power is neutral, and the dark and light side stem from the same source, then there can be no clear-cut line dividing good from evil.

As one Witchcraft practitioner says, "There is a law or rule in witchcraft which states that if you harm anyone without justification, then you can expect it to come back to you three-fold."[17] Note that he says "without justification." So if one can justify doing harm, then it is okay. Even those occultists who would disagree with this statement cannot defend anything beyond a subjective concept of harm or evil.

Now that you have a firm grasp of the concepts, get ready for the next section, where, one by one, I'll unpack occult beliefs and practices.

BRINGING IT HOME

The ideas in this chapter can be difficult to grasp. Try these activities to help your child understand more about good and evil and how they fit in the world of the paranormal.

- Draw a picture of the yin and yang symbol (or simply find one and show it to your child). Ask your child what he or she thinks it means. If your child is old enough to understand complex concepts, explain some of the popular meanings and ask your child to respond to each. (You'll find these earlier in the chapter, on page 65.)

- Ask: "Can there be a little bit of evil in good? Why or why not?" Read 1 John 1:7 together, which states that God is light and has no darkness at all. Then ask, "Can there be evil in God? Is there absolute good if it has evil in it? Why do you think that?"

- Read and talk about the story in Genesis 3. Ask your children: Did Eve and Adam decide the fruit tree was good? What were they doing when they decided the fruit was "good for food," even though God had forbidden it? Get your child to think about who decides what is good and evil.

- Ask: If good can be mixed with evil, then how do we know what is good? You can illustrate this by mixing two colors together. Use crayons or water-color paints with younger children. Explain that one color represents good (say, green) and another color (perhaps, orange) represents evil. After having your child mix the colors, ask: If these colors are always mixed, how do we know what is green or orange? If good and evil are always mixed, how do we know which is which?

PART TWO:

WHAT ASPECTS OF THE PARANORMAL DO OUR KIDS ENCOUNTER?

WHERE DIVINATION, SORCERY, AND SPIRIT CONTACT TOUCH OUR KIDS

6

WHAT'S YOUR SIGN?
THE MYSTIQUE
AND MISTAKE OF
ASTROLOGY

*E*xpress your zodiac sign with this collectible Barbie doll! Inspired by the twelve signs of the zodiac, Barbie doll personifies the mystique and personalized appeal of your astrological sign. This absolutely beautiful doll is part of an exclusive line created only for Wal-Mart and Walmart.com.[1]

- Zodiac Barbie is wearing a simple flowing gown with a satin ribbon tie-around belt at her waist.

- The gown is decorated with the Cancer zodiac sign.

- Zodiac Barbie is also wearing a faux fur shawl to complete her ensemble.

- She is wearing a charm bracelet with the Cancer zodiac symbol charm.[2]

WHAT IS ASTROLOGY?

Horoscope columns appear in almost every newspaper, usually near the comics section, and in most women's and girls' magazines. Millions read horoscopes every day looking for fun, yet also for advice.

Astrology is not astronomy, which is the scientific study of space, heavenly bodies, and galaxies. Astronomy tells us, for example, that Mars is a certain size and certain distance from Earth, while astrology claims that Mars represents energy, strength, aggression, passion, and impulse. Astronomy is information based on measurements, scientific theory, and objective data, while astrology is based on esoteric interpretations of the meaning of the planets, zodiac signs, and planetary positions.

Horoscope columns are based on astrology, but astrology is more than the horoscope columns in the newspapers and in magazines. Astrology is a form of divination using the sun, moon, and planets to give information on the past, present, or future. Astrology is an occult practice rooted in ancient Babylon. It originated, historians believe, when the ancient Chaldeans observed the orderly movement of the planets and assigned them godlike character and powers. The planets eventually were worshipped as gods. Each planet came to be the ruler of certain areas of life. The astrologers, who advised kings and rulers, interpreted the pattern of planets as omens or signs of what was to come.

By integrating psychological terms and Eastern beliefs, such as karma[3] and reincarnation,[4] contemporary astrology shifted in the twentieth century from fatalistic readings and predictions to a tool of character analysis and spiritual advice. Although future events are still part of the chart reading, they are downplayed and are usually called "forecasting" or "upcoming trends."

Astrology is based on the belief that the planetary

positions at one's birth time and birthplace reflect that person's character, lessons in life, challenges, and spiritual path. Most astrologers, like all occultists, believe that since a mystical force connects the universe and everyone in it, our intimate journeys can be read in external factors, such as the planets. This belief is stated in the occult expression, "As above, so below." The planetary positions are the divination tool the astrologer uses to "see" the person's character, potential abilities, issues, life path, and even past life issues.

Reading an astrological chart is technical and extremely complex. The planets are placed in a circle divided into twelve sections, called houses, around which fall the 360 degrees of a fixed zodiac belt, Aries through Pisces. The astrologer synthesizes the position of the planets by sign and house, the position of the planets in relation to each other, rulerships of the houses, the elements (air, earth, water, and fire) that are represented, certain emphasized points in the chart, as well as other factors. These threads of the chart are tied together as the astrologer does the reading. Due to the rather open-ended meanings in a chart, a range of options is given. This is partly why astrology is so popular—the client is likely to relate to at least one of the options, thus adding a presumed validity to the reading.

Sometimes there is a psychic bonding between the astrologer and the chart. This bonding, similar to the altered state of mind achieved by mediums, channelers, psychics, or card readers, is the basis of many occult techniques. When I practiced astrology, I often felt what seemed to be a beam of energy connecting my mind to the chart and a "force" guiding me through the chart. I had been introduced to my "spiritual master" years earlier in a class through guided visualization.[5] Since the astrologer is engaging in an occult practice, the door opens wide for supernatural guidance apart from God.

Astrology is also used to answer questions. When a client asks a question, the astrologer notes the time and casts a chart for the time and place of the question. This is called *horary astrology* and has its own particular rules of chart interpretation in order to answer the question.

HOROSCOPES

Are those ubiquitous horoscope columns in the newspaper and magazines imaginary concoctions, as many believe? Horoscope columns are usually written by astrologers or by psychics with some knowledge of astrology. The column is divided into the twelve zodiac signs based on the position of the sun, such as Aries for March 20–April 19, Taurus for April 20–May 21, and so forth. The dates vary slightly from year to year. This solar position is called the sun sign and is what people refer to when they say their birth sign is Gemini or Capricorn or Leo. Those who write these columns believe that anyone can receive guidance by knowing the positions of the moon and the faster-moving planets, such as Mercury, Venus, Mars, and sometimes Jupiter, combined with the sun sign.

An astrologer consults an *ephemeris*, which gives the positions of the sun, moon, and planets and notes where they will be at certain times and on certain dates. The astrologer might observe that on a certain day the moon will be in Gemini, Mercury will be in Scorpio, Venus in Libra, and Mars in Virgo, and the astrologer will then integrate those factors for each person's sun sign. Those factors will interact differently for each of the various sun signs. The moon is especially important for daily horoscopes since it changes signs every two and a half days. This kind of astrology is not the same as reading a birth chart, but rather focuses on dispensing daily advice and information for the twelve zodiac signs based on the faster-moving planets. Though many professional astrologers frown on horoscope columns as watered-down astrology, horoscopes are nevertheless a form of astrology.

See what I mean about the complexity of reading an astrological chart? Even if you don't fully understand all of this, you can see at the very least that a horoscope is more than simply someone's idea of an innovative advice column. Astrology is a serious belief system.

THE ZODIAC SNARE

The zodiac Barbie dolls and hundreds of other toys and objects based on the sun signs are intended to appeal to children who have the same zodiac sign. For example, a girl who was born under the sign of Aries would identify with the Barbie Aries doll or a bracelet with the Aries symbol. Younger children are drawn into a fascination with astrology often through their association with the zodiac sign.

Those zodiac signs take on more significance as children get older. When people ask, "What's your sign?" they're implicitly acknowledging that the characteristics associated with each sign are valid and true. Telling a young girl she is a Virgo (someone who is detail-oriented and health-conscious, according to zodiac basics) may cause her to see herself that way to the detriment of other abilities. She may (consciously or subconsciously) imitate what she believes are the traits of Virgo, even if she does not naturally have them.

Another danger is developing a dependency on reading horoscopes. If a horoscope happens to be correct one day, the person may have even more desire to read the horoscope the next day, and on succeeding days. In a short time, this person can develop a reliance on the advice given. The words of the column wend their way into the subconscious as well as the conscious, making it easy to accept as a predictive truth that maybe "Today you need to confront a friend" or "Today is a good day to be alone." This advice can influence decisions and actions, perhaps to the detriment of the reader or those around him or her.

I have talked to many Christians, young and old alike, who told me they read their horoscope every day and can't imagine doing without it. I have a hunch they are perhaps secretly hoping that there is something to it, even if they are not conscious of this. When children are told that reading a horoscope is okay if they're just doing it for fun, this doesn't prevent them from believing it, and it certainly does not prevent a growing interest in astrology.

People like hearing about themselves and they enjoy things that seem tailored especially for them. It makes them feel special. However, what astrology really does is dehumanize people; it puts them into artificial and arbitrary classifications so that people see themselves only in terms of the zodiac.

In many ways, the zodiac is a snare, with each sign a bit of bait, luring the mind and spirit away from God to false beliefs.

IS ASTROLOGY TRUE?

Many people come to believe there is something to astrology because they see truth in the personality descriptions of their zodiac sign. This is selective thinking: identifying with the traits of a particular sign while dismissing the ones that are not accurate. For every person who thinks that Leo really describes who he or she is, at least a hundred people born with the sun sign Leo do not fit the Leo paradigm at all.

The astrological zodiac arbitrarily divides up personality traits that all humans have in common. Everyone can identify with many traits from many zodiac signs. Professional astrologers are the first to dismiss classifying someone solely by the zodiac (or "sun") sign, since they believe that a person is made up of all the planetary signs in the chart. If professional astrologers don't even accept sun signs as valid, why should anyone else believe that there is any truth to the description?

Astrology can have the ring of scientific truth. However, the view of astrology as science has several strikes against it.

The zodiac belt (the constellations of Aries, Taurus, Gemini, etc.) is a fixed, artificial pattern that is no longer accurate. Over the years, and due to the earth's wobble in its rotation, the zodiac constellations have moved several degrees relative to the earth. So if your birth date makes you Libra, there is a chance that you are *actually* Virgo, or if you are Aquarius, you might be Capricorn, and so on.

Different astrologers use different "house systems" to compute the twelve houses of the astrological chart, which usually results in different setups for the same chart. Most astrology used in the West is geocentric, that is, it is based on the planets as though they are moving around the earth rather than the sun. Heliocentric charts, based on the planets moving around the sun, show the position of Earth as one of the planets. Although some astrologers do heliocentric charts, it is not the most common form.

Astrologers have answers to all of these concerns, but these answers come from a worldview that astrology is based on a higher or more accurate form of knowledge than mundane knowledge. Esoteric knowledge, in the view of occultists, always trumps objective knowledge. Also, since astrologers deem that astrology is an ancient art and that it works, any data showing it to be false is dismissed. Many astrologers believe that astrology operates on a higher law than science, and that one day, science will catch up to and confirm astrology.

WHAT ABOUT THE MAGI?

Matthew 2 tells of the Magi who visit the young Jesus, bringing him frankincense, myrrh, and gold. The Magi were probably part of a Persian caste of priests and wise men, expert in mathematics, interpreting dreams and signs, and the study of the stars.[6] They were advisers to kings and rulers.[7] Astronomy, the scientific study of the heavenly bodies, and astrology, the occult interpretation of the position and movement of the stars (and planets), were one and the same at that time. Therefore, the Magi were probably practicing a mixture of astronomy and astrology.

This Scripture passage does not give much information on the star that the Magi saw. Contemporary astronomers have tried to determine if there was a particular astronomical event in the time period when it is believed Jesus was born that would account for an unusual or bright configuration, but so far they have uncovered nothing satisfactory. The exact time of Jesus' birth is not known, which makes it harder to find such an astronomical event. Matthew 2:9 states that the star "rested" or "stood" over the house where Jesus was. A natural star or planet cannot actually stand over such a specific or small location.

Some theories suggest that because of the Jewish captivity in Babylon, the Magi knew the prophetic passage in Numbers 24:17 predicting a "star" arising out of Jacob. However, it is unclear whether or not the passage is referring to a physical star; it seems instead to refer to the symbolic representation of a king. No astronomical or astrological information is given.

Some Bible scholars believe that the star was an unusually bright light, the Shekinah—the light of the glory of God—the same light that was the pillar of fire for the Israelites in the desert and the fire seen by Moses in the burning bush. Perhaps the light appeared as an unusual star to the Magi just as God's presence appeared as a pillar of fire in the wilderness. It is also possible that the star was a supernatural star created by God that he used to lead the Magi to Christ.

The star first led the Magi to Herod in Jerusalem, not to Christ. It seems from the passage that the Magi had either lost track of the star or the star had disappeared, since they had to ask Herod, "Where is the one who has been born King of the Jews?" Herod's chief priests and scribes indicated that the Jewish prophecy foretold the birth of a ruler in Bethlehem. In this way, the birth of Jesus was announced to Herod and his court, and they were put on notice about a fulfilled prophecy. The Magi left and the star once again guided them—this time to Jesus.

The account of the Magi and the unusual star rests solidly between accounts of other supernatural events, showing God's hand in the birth of Jesus. Matthew 1:18–25 tells about Mary's conception of Jesus by the Holy Spirit, and God's angel visiting Joseph in a dream. In the passage following the Magi's visit to Jesus, Matthew 2:12–15, an angel warns the Magi in a dream not to return to Herod, and an angel again appears in Joseph's dream, warning him of Herod's plan to slay the child and telling him to take Mary and Jesus to Egypt.

There is no indication that astrology was used to find Jesus, although the Magi undoubtedly practiced the kind of astrology used then to counsel rulers. It's significant to note, too, that the Magi, who journeyed from a pagan culture, were the first people recorded to worship Jesus (Matthew 2:11).

WHY ASTROLOGY SEEMS TO WORK

Astrology, since it presents so many options, seems to offer something for everyone. When an astrologer predicts the future, usually this prediction is given in generalized terms. For example, an astrologer might say, "You are likely to have some unexpected job changes in the next six months that will be upsetting to you." Although the astrologer may be getting this information through interpretation of an astrological chart, it is likely that something could happen that would seem to fulfill this.

Most contemporary astrologers do not believe that astrology can exactly predict events. The terms usually used by astrologers when talking about future events are "trends" or "forecasting." Astrologers believe that the indicators of coming events in the birth chart represent "energies" or influences coming into the life of the person, which they may use in different ways, or even ignore.

Most clients want to believe the astrologer. A client has usually paid money, invested time, and perhaps hoped for useful information or guidance. No one wants to be disappointed, so people naturally latch on to anything the astrologer says that sounds correct or helpful.

Selective memory allows the client to forget anything the astrologer said that was wrong and recall only the things that were right. And let's not rule out simple coincidence as a reason for the apparent accuracy of astrology.

There's one other possibility—and it's the most unsettling. Since the astrologer is practicing a forbidden occult art, it is possible that demonic activity is involved. It is possible that fallen angels could have access to knowledge about the client's past or present, or to other "unknown" information, and could provide that to an astrologer. Astrologers who are aware of their spirit guides or "guiding angels" often believe in supernatural guidance, though they wouldn't claim that this guidance comes from demons. Yet no matter what the astrologer may believe, demonic help cannot be ruled out.

WHY ASTROLOGY IS WRONG

Astrology is a form of divination, and God has strong words against divination, as seen in Deuteronomy 18, Isaiah 47:13–15, and indirectly in Deuteronomy 4:19 and 17:3. There is danger in cultivating an interest in astrology through reading the horoscope, zodiac dolls, or jewelry or other items. These things lend credibility to astrology and give it an aura of harmless fun.

Some may discount horoscope columns or astrology as silly or fraudulent, but having been involved in it myself for several years, I can vouch for the ways it can negatively affect one's worldview. For example, it can lead even a casual participant to analyze people and events through the filter of astrology.

Like all occult tools, astrology ties one into the spirit world, whether desired by the practitioner or not. Two former astrologers who are now Christians, Karen Winterburn and Charles Strohmer, attest to this. Winterburn states that she progressed from using astrology as a "neutral" tool into spirit contact, and that she discovered this was true for all successful astrologers whom she knew.[8] According to Strohmer, the astrology chart is "the mediumistic point of interaction" for the astrologer, just as a crystal ball is for a psychic.[9] This was also true for me: I experienced guidance from spirit beings as I read the charts.

Looking at astrological signs for identity, horoscopes for advice, or an astrological reading for information are disobeying God. Astrologers assert they are not worshipping the planets. Yet looking to the positions and supposed meanings of the planets, sun, and moon is a form of worship because it honors an esoteric system as opposed to honoring and obeying God.

The bottom line is that astrology is pseudoscience and is not based on objective data, but rather on occult beliefs that the planets hold hidden meanings. And it is not from God.

BRINGING IT HOME

Use these ideas to help your child understand the truth about astrology.

- Ask your child if he or she reads the horoscope. If so, what would happen if it were right one day? Would this cause him or her to want to read it more? Talk with your child about the lure of the horoscope.

- Ask: If the horoscope turns out right for someone, does it mean that it was right for everyone on that day born under that sign? How could that be possible? Since it will have to be wrong for some of these people, can it truly be accurate?

- Ask your child if he thinks all people can be classified into twelve types. Talk to your child about how it would be if God decided there were only twelve types of people and everybody had to fit into those categories. Point out how this takes away from the unique personality, appearance, and talents the Lord has given us.

- Have your child read Isaiah 47:13–15 and Deuteronomy 4:19 and 17:3 and discuss how these passages show God's view of astrology, and what it means to be looking to the heavens for guidance, instead of seeking him.

7

WHO ARE THE PSYCHICS AND CAN THEY HELP?

Would it be sin to practice telepathy, or improve my "psychic" ability using methods that have nothing to do with the occult such as numerology, tarot, etc.... If it is, then what kind of paranormal "power" if you will is not? If it isn't, then how would you suggest that I practice my psychic awareness and ability? I am only a teen, and I am very interested by the paranormal, but I do not want it to interfere in any way with my religion.[1]

Not long ago, psychic hotlines were advertised frequently on television. Although those days have gone, the psychics have not. Psychics are presented often in movies and on television as people who help others. Television shows feature psychics who have helped the police. There's a talk show that includes a regular segment with psychic and medium Sylvia Browne, who answers questions from the audience. Psychic hotlines may have cooled, but psychics are still as "hot" as ever.

The term *psychic* (some also use the term *clairvoyant*, which means "to see clearly") is a general term that refers to actions such as the following:

1. Doing readings merely by "seeing" the issues through their psychic powers

2. Contacting the dead

3. Channeling spirits (allowing the spirit to speak through them)

4. Using divination tools such as tarot cards to receive information

5. Claiming psychic powers are scientific (may use the term *parapsychology*)

Psychics are everywhere. You may have noticed a recent interest in pet psychics, people who claim to be able to know the thoughts and feelings of animals. And while not all those who contact the dead or use divination tools call themselves psychics, they would undoubtedly claim to have psychic powers.

Psychic Powers

Have you heard the terms *sixth sense* or *parapsychology*? Or maybe *second sight*, *ESP*, or *the third eye*? These terms have become part of our culture and usually are just other names for psychic powers.

Psychic powers are thought to be supernatural or paranormal abilities that can be used to gather or receive information. Many psychics believe that everyone has latent or hidden psychic powers, and that these abilities only need to be developed. The theory that we use only 10 percent of the brain is often repeated by psychics and those sympathetic to psychic phenomena and other supernormal powers. However, this 10 percent claim is an urban myth based on faulty data and has been discredited for some time. It is simply not true.[2] Actually, during any typical day, everybody uses most of the brain.[3]

A popular term that became fashionable in the 1970s, *ESP* (extra sensory perception), described the supernatural ability to sense or know things. Duke University in North Carolina is well-known for its studies and experiments on what is called *parapsychology*, which covers supposed abilities like ESP and other forms of paranormal activities, sometimes referred to as psychokinetic phenomena.

Many academics who study this area believe these phenomena are projections and expressions of the unconscious, although this still requires an element of belief in the paranormal to accept this idea. *Psychokinesis* is a term for moving objects with the mind (or the unconscious) and is not possible physically; therefore, it also falls in the category of the paranormal. ESP and psychic powers are virtually the same, though attempts to present ESP as scientific have elevated it above the term psychic.

The *third eye* refers to the area between the eyes where, according to Hindu yoga teachings, the sixth *chakra* is located. A chakra is allegedly an invisible wheel of energy through which a force called *kundalini*, coiled like a serpent at the base of the spine (according to Hindu beliefs), rises through the body, awakening one to spiritual insight and awareness. This particular chakra is alleged to be the center of psychic powers or the ability to see psychically, that is, without physical vision. One writer cites yoga as calling the third eye "the seat of human consciousness and the point of contact between mind and spirit."[4] Due to the great increase in the popularity of yoga, the belief in chakras is growing.

Those who claim to have psychic powers claim different types. *Telepathy* is the paranormal ability to send or receive a thought over distance without verbal or visual help, and can also mean knowing what someone else is thinking at the moment; *clairaudience* (literally, "hearing clearly") is being able to hear something without using the sense of hearing; and *clairvoyance* is being able to see something without using the eyes.

Psychometry is "reading" an object and getting information about the owner or circumstances connected to the object merely by touching or holding it. *Precognition* is the ability to see and tell the future (this is also claimed by some who use divinatory tools, such as astrology and reading cards).

LEARNING TO BE PSYCHIC

When I took psychic-development classes before I was a Christian, we were taught specific techniques to grow our abilities. We brought objects to class to learn psychometry; we sat across from a classmate and focused on being receptive to psychic information in an effort to "read" that person; we practiced seeing things in our minds in order to develop psychic sensitivity; and we looked at a class member standing against a white wall and tried to see his aura, a supposed energy field that surrounds every person. If there were any "hits," we were excited, and convinced we were developing these latent powers. Naturally, no one took much note of the failures or kept track of them in contrast to the successes.

In addition to these techniques, we were taught that all people have spirits hovering around them and guiding them; we were introduced to reincarnation;[5] we learned that the twelve disciples of Jesus each represented one of the twelve astrological signs; we participated in séances, sessions to contact the dead; we were told that we all can achieve Christ Consciousness,[6] and that we are all the I AM. As you can see, learning these practices was accompanied by specific spiritual views. The teachings I mentioned here are just the tip of the iceberg in the realm of psychic phenomena.

One of the most critical teachings was about how to go into an altered or meditative state. I had already learned some Hindu, Tibetan Buddhist, and Zen Buddhist meditation methods and had been practicing them, so this was not difficult for me. Most psychics believe that going into such a state, which is actually a self-induced hypnotic trance, allows the person to overcome the rationality of the mind and thereby be receptive to the information given through psychic channels, by spirits, by Spirit,[7] or by whomever the psychic believes is the source of information.

Some psychics go into deep trances during which they become a *channel* or vehicle for a spirit speaking through them. This is called *channeling*. In the lighter trance state, one is still aware of the surroundings and is still operating in a conscious, albeit altered, state. In the deeper trance of channeling, one is not aware of his or her surroundings and usually does not recall what happened during the time of being "out." Channeling is not as popular as it once was, although it is still practiced.[8] A popular form of channeling is through writing rather than speaking. This is called automatic writing and is discussed in the next chapter.

Once these techniques for altered states are mastered, it becomes easy to "slip" in and out of such a state at will. Where do psychics think the information comes from? Not all psychics agree, but generally they believe one or more of the following:

- They are tapping into an energy field, which contains the information.

- They are accessing a type of psychic central records division called the Akashic Record, which contains all information about the past, present, and future.

- They are receiving the information from the client's higher self who has access to information pertinent to that client.

- The information is coming from the psychic's spirit guide or from God.

THE WHITE LIGHT

When a person takes steps to develop psychic abilities, he or she is opening the door to fearful experiences. As my psychic abilities expanded, so did the frightening experiences. This was true for many of my friends and associates in the occult as well. It is common practice for a psychic to call on benevolent protective forces or to visualize "white light" before practicing a psychic technique, doing a reading, or engaging in spirit contact.

There is a belief that visualizing a white light will bring protection. By doing this, psychics acknowledge the existence of evil or harmful beings. This raises valid questions, such as: How do they know the "benevolent" beings are not evil and merely disguising themselves as benevolent spirits or guides? What law says a white light is a barrier to evil entities? Why would such a light keep out any spirits? God's Word reveals that even Satan disguises himself as an "angel of light" (2 Corinthians 11:14).

DIFFERENT LABELS, SAME OLD STUFF

Psychic power is promoted under other names, usually in an attempt to appear scientific. One of these terms is *remote viewing* (RV), a term for seeing persons, objects, or events without using physical senses or equipment at a location or time remote from the viewer. Proponents try to make it sound scientific, but they offer no valid proof. The fact that several newspaper stories appeared in the 1990s revealing that the U.S. government had used remote viewers in the Cold War has given RV some credibility. Supporters of RV have claimed that results show it works. However, psychic abilities can garner "hits," either by coincidence or through information from demons; and since the criteria for a Christian should not be *results* when it comes to the use of psychic abilities, Christians should not be impressed by these hits.

Several Internet Web sites offer information supporting another form of psychic power, *psi*. Based on my e-mail inbox, this has apparently attracted a number of teens. There is no secret about what *psi* is. *Psi* is the first letter of the Greek word *psyche*, and designates forms of ESP and other areas associated with parapsychology. One Web site states: "We are the international professional organization of scientists and scholars engaged in the study of *psi* (or 'psychic') experiences, such as telepathy, clairvoyance, psychokinesis, psychic healing, and precognition."[9] Because scientists and scholars claim to be involved, and because this group engages in studies, a veneer of scientific decorum coats these blatant paranormal activities, misleading many, including Christians, into believing there is an objective basis to these powers.

TEEN PSYCHIC

It's great to encourage your children to read, but how would you respond if you found your teen or preteen reading about contacting spirits, learning the path of the shaman, or exploring spiritual empowerment? This is all offered in *Teen Psychic: Exploring Your Intuitive Spiritual Powers,* a book written for teens, which offers spiritual views based on experiencing feelings, trusting the inner self or inner wisdom, and various entities who act as benevolent guides in one's quest.[10]

The book's subtitle calls for exploring intuition, but the book goes beyond that into the realm of psychic beliefs and practices, Buddhist worldviews, accessing energy, shamanistic spirit contact and beliefs, obtaining a spirit guide, and step-by-step meditation instructions. In this one book, the author essentially sums up the immense amount of learning and reading I did over a period of several years when getting involved in New Age, Eastern, and occult beliefs in the 1970s and '80s.

Each chapter is prefaced with two brief narratives: the personal story of a teen who has gained an insight or overcome a challenge, and a tale or fable from an indigenous culture that teaches a principle or moral from a pagan worldview. The author refers to these characters and lessons as she instructs the reader on that particular theme. The teachings encourage readers to believe in themselves and to trust their own instincts and supposed inner wisdom. This is appealing to teens going through the dramatic peaks and valleys of adolescence and to those young people struggling with self-image issues.

An example will illustrate what this book is teaching. Chapter 7, "The Path of the Visionary," begins with the story of Scott, a high school senior who goes on a vision quest and has a dream that reveals him as someone with shamanic vision. He trusted his spirit and "heard its call."[11] He found courage and the belief he could succeed in following his dreams. A myth of the Carib shamans in Suriname follows Scott's account. This tells of a young boy who, as he is instructed by his teachers, has visions, contacts spirits, is then invaded by some violent spirits, gets wisdom from other spirits, and realizes he is now a shaman.

Johnson draws from these two tales to teach the reader that everybody has a higher self within, and an available external power or spirit that speaks to everyone every day. She advises the reader to open doors to the spirit world for healing, and she presents a meditation during which the teen reader is to contact her spirit guide. The chapter continues with information on dream yoga, meeting animal spirits, going into a trance, and specific steps on doing automatic writing. Johnson states that the spirit guide can be Christ, an angel, or an ancestor.[12]

And this is just one of many books targeted to teens on this subject.

IF PSYCHICS HELP THE POLICE, AREN'T THEY GOOD?

Some TV shows feature stories of psychics who help the police in finding criminals or missing people. Perhaps more than any other representation in the media, this gives children and teens the idea that being a psychic must be a good thing. Let's consider several things here:

1.   How true is the story?

2.   Is the psychic giving specific information that leads immediately to the solution?

3.   How does the psychic get the information?

4.   What criteria should be used to evaluate this situation?

First of all, the viewer doesn't know how true the story is about the psychic helping the police. Many television shows overdramatize these accounts and may even change facts in order to present an exciting story. Usually the viewer has no way to check out the facts, so one should not assume the report is necessarily true.

In many cases, the psychic is giving general information. For example, the psychic might say the body is near water or in a wooded area. Well, people who have been missing a long time are often dead, and it would not be terribly surprising if their bodies have been lost or hidden in a lake or river, or in an isolated or remote spot such as the woods. Other clues are often tied in later. For example, the psychic might say she sees the number 2 and the letters p and a. These could be tied into the missing person later, should he or she be found, in many ways: perhaps in the name of a lake, town, business, or highway in the vicinity of the body.

Let's say a missing person's body is found and the nearest road is Highway 2 and the nearest business is Pat's Lunch Place. The psychic might point out that this ties in with the number and letters she saw.

Is this information enough to find the body? Not at all! Normally, the body is found another way and then these "clues" are tied in later. Most tie-ins are merely coincidental. After all, the alphabet has only twenty-six letters, and numbers only go from zero to nine, and combinations thereof. Even a broken clock is right twice a day.

What if the information is very specific and does lead to a solution? As seen with astrology, this could be evidence of demonic help. You may be wondering if demons can give such information, why are psychics not *always* successful in giving the information needed by police? I believe God does not allow the demons to do this, because he limits them just as he limits Satan.

According to one magazine article, some police departments consult psychics, either at the request of the family of the victim or "more often out of sheer desperation as a case grows cold."[13] One psychic acknowledges that psychics are "not crime solvers," but "investigative tools."[14] Despite the successes claimed by psychics, former FBI profiler Clint Van Zandt stated that in his twenty-five years with the FBI, "I never saw a psychic provide anything but information so general that it was useless in the case."[15]

The article admits that most law-enforcement officials are not convinced psychics can help in investigations. After all, look at all the unsolved cases still on the books. Why are psychics not rushing to police stations or calling the media with the locations of people still missing or the names of killers in unsolved murders?

The way to evaluate such situations is not whether the psychic is giving correct information, but to look at what God's Word has to say. Whether something works or not in the context of the paranormal is not the right criteria. Such things should be rejected even if they appear good or useful to the world.

PROPHETS AND PSYCHICS: GIFTS FROM GOD?

Many psychics claim their gift is from God. And what about biblical prophecy? God's prophets did not use psychic ability, but were given their information directly by God in words or visions. The prophets did not seek to develop supernormal powers. God chose the prophets and gave them revelation. Most importantly, biblical prophecy glorified God and proclaimed his Word. Messages given by psychics do not lead others toward conviction of sin, need for salvation only through Jesus Christ, or to belief in the Bible as God's Word, but rather further away, often blatantly denying the Bible and Christian doctrine.

God gives the acid test for prophecy and predictions in Deuteronomy 18:21–22: If the prophecy is not 100 percent accurate, the prophet is not from God. In my psychic-development classes, the psychics used to tell us that a really *good* psychic on his or her *best day* might be about 85 percent accurate. No psychic claims 100 percent accuracy 100 percent of the time. Therefore, a psychic "gift" is not prophecy, and it isn't from God.

In Deuteronomy 13:1–3, God makes it clear that even if someone gives accurate information or foretells an event that comes true, but then leads us away from the biblical God, we must reject that prophet (or in this case, psychic). There is no way around it: When psychic ability is put to the test, it fails.

WARNING

Consulting a psychic, in person or by phone, for fun or out of curiosity, should be avoided. As with astrology, it is tempting to start using the psychic as a way to cope and make decisions. Many have ended up relying on the psychic as a counselor to listen to their problems. Don't take psychics lightly, or your child may believe there is nothing really wrong with consulting one.

The prophet Daniel, when interpreting the king's dream, said it best: "No wise man, enchanter, magician or diviner can explain to the king the mystery he has asked about, but there is a God in heaven who reveals mysteries" (Daniel 2:27–28 NIV). For it is God who "alone has all wisdom and power," and who "reveals deep and mysterious things and knows what lies hidden in darkness, though he himself is surrounded by light" (Daniel 2:20, 22 NLT).

An extension of the topic on psychics is divination, often called "fortune-telling." Is someone who gazes into a crystal ball merely a cartoon joke? Well, actually, real people do that, and the term for this is *scrying*. The next chapter will introduce you to that and many other tools and types of divination, such as tarot cards, numerology, and pendulums.

BRINGING IT HOME

Use these ideas to help your child understand the difference between a biblical prophet and a psychic. Going through this exercise will model for your child how to use God's Word to measure questionable activities.

- Choose a biblical prophet such as Elijah, Daniel, or John the Baptist. Read about this prophet and ask your child to point out where God shows that this prophet received his abilities from the Lord. In the story of Daniel, for example, look at Daniel 2:27 where Daniel acknowledges the Lord as the One who gives him his knowledge and who knows all things.

- Read Deuteronomy 18:21–22, which gives the test for a prophet. Ask your child what he thinks of psychics who admit they are wrong some of the time, and that people have noticed no psychic is ever 100 percent correct. Ask your child to compare this to what you just read about prophets.

8

DIVINATION— NOT DIVINE!

*H*ow many times have you seen cartoons of turbaned psychics reading crystal balls? This figure has become such a stock character for jokes and stories that it may seem unreal. However, although scam artists sit at crystal balls, read your palm, or read cards, others do these things seriously, and they are practicing an art that goes back to ancient times.

Divination is the practice of obtaining information using a means beyond the natural or by reading hidden meaning into ordinary patterns or objects. Two forms have already been discussed: astrology and psychic abilities. The Bible terms for *divination* may be translated as "witchcraft," "soothsaying," or other terms. First Samuel 15:23 asserts that "rebellion is as the sin of divination." God compares rebellion to divination because divination is seeking supernatural direction from a source other than God.

The Old Testament records a variety of methods of divination: a cup (Genesis 44:5), examining the livers of dead animals (Ezekiel 21:21), interpretation of dreams (Daniel), casting down arrows (Ezekiel 21:21), using rods (Hosea 4:12), consulting household idols, consulting the dead (necromancy), and astrology (Isaiah 47:13). These diviners were called false prophets, and their practices were aligned with witchcraft and condemned by God (Deuteronomy 18:10; 1 Samuel 15:23; and Jeremiah 27:9).[1] Other passages against divination include 2 Kings 17:17; 21:6; 2 Chronicles 33:6; Isaiah 2:6; and Ezekiel 13:23.

The term most often used today for divination is fortune-telling, but this word is vague and implies that the person is mainly telling the future. This was true in the past, but much of modern divination focuses on the person's past, present, and future career path, relationships, money issues, health, and other areas of life. It is common to refer to a divination session as a "reading." Depending on who is doing the reading, it can appear almost like a counseling session. The modern fortune-teller has several tools at his or her disposal.

GAZING INTO THE CRYSTAL BALL

Is there really anything going on in the crystal ball? No, it's not a miniature video screen playing out scenes as often depicted in cartoons. A crystal ball is merely a tool for focusing. By gazing into it, images or words supposedly arise in the gazer's mind and are simultaneously reflected in the crystal ball. A crystal ball really isn't necessary—one can gaze into any shiny surface such as a mirror, body of water, or opaque glass. The gazing may induce an altered state of consciousness, bringing about a vision, or call forth a psychic picture. This form of divination is called *scrying* and those who practice it most likely would be psychics, witches, or Wiccans. One of my teachers in a psychic development class told us that if we gazed into a mirror by the light of a candle, we would see our face change into the faces we had in past lives. Although these methods are recent variations, scrying itself is an ancient practice of divination.

NUMBER, PLEASE

Numerology is a form of divination using numbers to represent hidden meanings. Names are converted to numbers through a system in which each letter of the alphabet corresponds to a number up to 9 (the number 1 represents the letter *a*, 2 is for the letter *b*, etc., through the letter *i*, which is a 9, then it starts over at 1 again for *j*, and resumes). Names and birth dates are usually reduced to a one-digit number through an addition process and a casting out of nines. For example, June 5, 1954, would be a 3. This is derived from 6 for June as the sixth month + 5 + 1 (the 9 is cast out of "1954" and 5 + 4 = 9, which is cast out, leaving 1), which = 12. And 12 is 1 + 2, equaling a final number of 3. This number allegedly shows a life path or destiny. The numerologist interprets numbers for the person's birth date and name, often in a psychological and spiritual manner. Numerology is commonly used in conjunction with other forms of divination, such as astrology and tarot cards.

An ancient numerological practice called *gematria* assigns a numerical value to the alphabet, discovering the number for each word, and then comparing it to other words with the same numerical value in order to see hidden relationships and patterns. This goes back to ancient Greece, the Gnostics, and perhaps even to Babylon. A Hebrew practice of gematria is based on a mystical view of the actual Hebrew words: "The assumption behind this technique is that numerical equivalence is not coincidental. Since the world was created through God's 'speech,' each letter represents a different creative force."[2] This practice became more common within Kabbalah, an esoteric teaching based on the belief that the Torah, the first five books of the Old Testament, is an encrypted code.

Arithmancy is an earlier form of numerology practiced by the Chaldeans and the Greeks. Arithmancy is one of the subjects studied by Harry Potter and his schoolmates at the school for wizards, Hogwarts. In the fifth book, Harry gives Hermione a book on numerology, which thrills her. Googling *arithmancy* one day, I came across an online article, purportedly by Hermione, on this topic.[3]

In this article, the fictional Hermione enthusiastically recommends using numbers to predict the future, and even gives instructions. She says that it is "almost scientific" and continues, "Predicting the future can be used in conjunction with other forms of magic to increase your power or chances of success. For example, if you're going to make a love potion for someone you fancy, wouldn't it be helpful to know what day they're more likely to be in a receptive mood?"

The Web site hosting the article is actually a Web site for witches. Any child who is a fan of Harry Potter and is curious about the word *arithmancy* could easily come across this article. It was on the first page that came up when I Googled the term. Not only will the child get validation for the belief in numerology, but she will also be taken to a Witchcraft Web site.

Although certain numbers are repeated in the Bible, such as seven, twelve, and forty, and significance may be derived from them in context, these numbers are never presented as representing a hidden meaning, nor does God specifically point out that these are special numbers. He simply uses them within recurrent themes, such as forty days and nights of rain for the flood, forty years in the wilderness for Moses, forty days in the desert for Jesus, and so on. This does not mean the numbers have any special significance outside the context in which they are given. Just because forty years and forty days are connected to Moses and Jesus, this does not mean one must go on a retreat for forty days (or forty years!), though it is perfectly fine to do so as long as one does not believe this is *required*, or that something special must result from it.

PENDULUMS AND SIMILAR DEVICES

Have you ever swung a needle or pencil at the end of a thread or string over a pregnant woman's belly or wrist to see if she was going to have a boy or girl? Although this is done at baby showers in the guise of a fun game, it is essentially divination based on the pendulum. Thinking that an object can gather and pass on information is part of divinatory belief, because there is an assumption that a supernatural power or force is at work.

Hosea 4:12 contains a reference to an early form of the pendulum: "My people consult their wooden idol, and their diviner's wand informs them." This method was possibly of Chaldean origin and involved holding two rods upright, and while doing an incantation, letting the rods fall to the ground. The way in which the rods fell, whether forward, backward, to the right or left, had a certain meaning.[4]

The description of a course teaching the use of pendulums in a Spring 2005 flyer from the Department of Recreation and Leisure in Arlington, Virginia, reads, "Learn to use the pendulum as a divination tool, a healing tool, or to measure energy. A pendulum can answer personal questions, find lost objects, guide us in our food choices, or confirm 'gut instinct.' ... THIS IS A FUN AND AMAZING WORKSHOP!" Other courses on New Age and occult topics are being offered increasingly in this county's program and across the country.

Dowsing with a pendulum was even being offered as part of a course at a 2005 symposium for psychotherapists and social workers. The course, "Feng Shui from the Heart," explained that the dowsing technique would be used "to clear past energies from any location," including the ability to "clear" spaces from a distance using a floor plan. Attendees were asked to bring a pendulum and the floor plan of their home.[5] The concept of "clearing past energies" is an occult practice based on a belief in negative and positive energies that can be summoned or banished through techniques or rituals.

Dowsing rods, used to find water, precious metals, minerals, gems, or lost objects, are also tools of divination. Dowsing rods or sticks are sometimes called witching rods or divining rods. Though traditionally made from forked branches of a tree, they can also be pieces of wire or metal, or a small pendulum. There is no scientific basis to support that a stick can "find" anything or be drawn to water or precious metals. Studies have shown that chance is as good as dowsing rods when it comes to finding water.

Those who practice dowsing can offer no scientific or objective reason for why dowsing should work; instead, they usually believe that it works due to a mystical force or energy. An article on dowsing in a New Age magazine states that dowsing is a tool "for understanding the natural forces of the Universe, and for working knowingly with the Divine and with Nature," and that dowsing is "simply magic—real magic."[6]

Using an object in a supernatural or magical way in order to obtain information is divination. Both pendulums and dowsing rods are good examples of this.

AUTOMATIC WRITING

This is a form of both divination and spirit contact, specifically channeling, but will be included in this section because the spirit contact is not always done consciously, at least at first.

Automatic writing can occur with deliberate attempts or can seem to happen with no effort. While the person is writing (or typing), he or she begins to feel that someone or something is directing the pen or pencil (or fingers on a typewriter or computer keyboard). The late Ruth Montgomery, at one time a prominent journalist and president of the National Press Club, claimed that while she was typing one day in the 1970s, her typewriter started tapping out a message that she was not consciously typing. This was the beginning of messages she began receiving from what she called her "guides." Ms. Montgomery ended up writing several books with alleged messages from the guides. Ms. Montgomery would ask questions and the guides would provide answers through the typewriter. Ms. Montgomery eventually claimed to be receiving messages this way from dead relatives.[7]

New Age author Neale Donald Walsch, author of several best sellers, claims that his first book, *Conversations with God, Book One,* was the outcome of writing out questions in a time of crisis. In 1992, Walsch, unhappy and full of questions about why his life seemed to be a failure, wrote a letter to God with his questions. As he finished writing the last question, Walsch claims, the pen moved on its own and he found himself writing words as though taking dictation.[8] Walsch says God was dictating the responses, although he does not explain how he knew this.

After his initial success with several books, Walsch wrote *Conversations with God for Teens.* This book consists of questions teens sent to Walsch, which Walsch then posed to God, purportedly writing down God's replies. Many Christians bought this book before checking it out, assuming from the title that it was a Christian book, and in a few cases, discovered only after having given the books to teens that it was not.

It is important never to assume anything about a book from the title or even from a cursory glance through the book, especially if the words "God," "Jesus," or "Christ" are in the title or book. Much New Age and occult literature contains these words.

To give you a taste of some of the ideas presented in *Conversations with God for Teens,* consider these: God is a pool of energy; there is no certain age or time for sexual initiation; there is no right or wrong; we should "drop our thoughts"; we are in an illusion; man's main purpose is to remember that man is actually God; after death, man will lose his individual distinctions in "The Oneness," but then become individualized and be born again, a cycle to repeat for eternity; and God does not judge, condemn, or forgive, since there is nothing to forgive.

Additionally, "God" misquotes the Bible or uses biblical quotes out of context throughout the book. "God" massages egos by telling the teens they are God, but then he turns around to say that they have all been living in an illusion and cannot trust their own thinking and senses.[9] This book is pure spiritual poison.

Instructions on how to do automatic writing usually coach the person on how to go into a trance state. I was taught this in my psychic-development classes, though automatic writing did not work for me. Automatic writing is done to get messages from dead people, guides from other dimensions, angels, or other disembodied beings. Or, in Walsch's case, to receive messages from God.

Some people attempt to do this without any conscious thought of whom they might be contacting. They merely want to see what happens if they try it, or they want answers to questions and don't care how they get them. Automatic writing is dangerous and violates God's prohibition on both divination and spirit contact.

THE TAROT

Tarot cards are illustrated with symbolic pictures with alleged hidden meanings that can be interpreted by a card reader. Some believe the tarot first were introduced as playing cards in fourteenth-century France or in Italy, while others believe their origin is from the Roma people (Gypsies), brought from Chaldea to Egypt, into Israel, and then to Greece.[10] However, the origin of these cards, bound in legend and myth, is disputed and murky.

Tarot cards are used in present times for divination as well as "the cultivation of intuition and psychic ability."[11] The pictures on the cards are interpreted symbolically in an occult context and represent the soul's journey to spiritual awakening, or the individual becoming whole.[12] Occultists widely accept that the tarot have "occult powers."[13] The cards are also used as a personal meditation tool.

A typical tarot deck includes seventy-eight cards that are divided into the Major Arcana and the Minor Arcana. The Minor Arcana, made up of fifty-six cards, is divided into four suits, Pentacles, Wands, Cups, and Swords, which are usually linked to the four elements of earth, air, water, and fire. The Major Arcana is comprised of twenty-two cards with richly symbolic pictures, some of which are the Emperor, the Tower, Death, the Hanged Man, the Hierophant, the Lovers, the Chariot, the Sun, the Moon, Justice, Strength, the Devil, and others. The Major Arcana represent "astrological, numerological, and kabbalistic teachings of the ancients" and are based on "the legends, myths, philosophies, religions, and magic beliefs of the human race."[14]

Some believe that the twenty-two cards of the Major Arcana originally corresponded to the twenty-two paths on the Kabbalah Tree of Life and the twenty-two letters of the Hebrew alphabet.[15] However, this link to the Kabbalah and the Hebrew letters is a disputed one.[16]

The most popular deck is the Rider-Waite deck, developed first by occultist Arthur E. Waite, a member of the occult Hermetic Order of the Golden Dawn, and published by William Rider & Son, Ltd. in 1910. Waite based the meaning of his cards on his occult studies.

Walk into any large bookstore, especially the chain stores, and you will easily find decks of tarot cards for sale. In addition to the Rider-Waite deck, hundreds of other tarot decks are available, such as tarot for feminists, witches, practitioners of ritual magic (the Thoth deck devised by Aleister Crowley), decks with Native American themes, Celtic themes, goddess themes, fairy-tale themes, etc. While meandering through a small bookstore (a branch of one of the larger chain stores) in the summer of 2005, I found several of these tarot decks. The cards are illustrated with colorful and sometimes highly artistic images, which makes them appealing.

When a user lays out the cards for a reading, it is believed that the cards will "fall into positions that inevitably relate to the subject of the reading."[17] Those who do these readings believe in this because they believe everything in the universe is connected. Tarot card symbology is linked to numerology and astrology. Reading cards for divination purposes is called *cartomancy*.

Some of the decks, such as the Rider-Waite, have biblical imagery. This is perhaps due to the tarot's connection to the Kabbalah (there was also a purported "Christian" Kabbalah). Whatever the origins, this is not surprising, since it is actually quite common for occult views and objects to incorporate biblical imagery or statements. The occult is not a system totally distinct from anything familiar, but rather one built on that which is familiar and/or appears to be good.

PALM READING

Those who practice palmistry or *chiromancy*, the reading of the hand, believe that the lines and other marks on the hand, as well as the shape and length of the fingers and hand, reveal information about the person's life. Major lines include a head line, heart line, fate line, and life line. The left hand reveals what is given at birth for one's destiny, while the right hand (opposite for left-handed people) shows what has been accomplished. This divinatory art began, according to some, as far back as 3000 BC.

One Web site states, "Your palm is the blueprint of your life and once a line appears on your hand it never goes away. The brain is said to electromagnetically etch the lines on your hand in accordance with the events of your life."[18] Another source states that biblical support was sought to validate palm reading from passages such as Isaiah 49:16, Job 27:7, and Proverbs 3:16, passages in which palms are mentioned.[19] Here again is the usual attempt to intertwine the Bible with an occult practice in spite of the fact that these passages have nothing to do with reading palms.

RUNES

Runes, whose origins remain disputed, were possibly early symbols arising from the Latin alphabet that later became ascribed to Norse or Germanic languages, and were connected to magical rituals involving the worship of Norse gods. The symbols were first found as inscriptions on monuments, weapons, personal objects, and furniture.[20] Runes are another crossover tool used both for divination and for magic (sorcery).

It is thought the symbols were originally carved on wood.[21] In present-day use, the symbols are on small, smooth ceramic stones kept in a pouch, or drawn on cards. When I was an astrologer, my son saw a Rune set in a New Age bookstore and wanted them. The set contained a black velvet pouch, small, smooth stones with the runes carved on them, and a book to interpret them. Several months after I became a believer in Christ, my son came across this pouch with the Rune stones and solemnly declared they needed to be thrown away. Although not yet a believer, he had understood at age nine that if astrology was wrong, so was Rune divination.

A December 1998 magazine for teen girls, *Twist,* offered a section called "Discover your future with ... Rune Stones." The top of the article said, "Want a new way to predict your dating destiny? These mystical stones have been around for more than 2,000 years. And they're even better than tarot cards!"[22] A page of twenty-five perforated cards, each depicting a Rune symbol, accompanied the article. Instructions were given on how to shuffle, draw, and lay out the cards for three different types of readings. On the opposing page were the names and interpretations for the Runes. Undoubtedly, the meanings were adapted for teen girls interested in boys and dating. Nevertheless, this is not only an introduction to divination and Runes, but also an encouragement to use them. Note that the magazine promotes Runes as "better than tarot cards," blandly assuming their teen readers' familiarity with tarot.

Runes are also used for magic. Therefore, Runes will also be covered in more detail in the chapter on magic.

THE I CHING

The I Ching is not hard to find in stores; it usually comes as a set of coins or sometimes cards marked with broken and unbroken lines. Many books offering advice on how to use the I Ching are available as well. The I Ching is also known as the Book of Changes and arises from the ancient religion of Taoism. The I Ching originally reflected the important Chinese concept of the relationship between heaven, earth, and man, referred to as "the three gifts." It is visually represented by patterns of three broken and unbroken lines called trigrams, which came to be carved on coins.

These coins eventually became a tool of divination based on the Taoist method of reading patterns of change in the universe and developed over a long period of time.[23] In place of coins, sometimes yarrow sticks were thrown.

The I Ching philosophy is based on the "concept of a unified and cyclical universe, in which the future develops according to fixed laws and numbers."[24] The trigrams later became sixty-four hexagrams with further commentaries added to the meaning of the patterns as the centuries passed, finally reaching the West in the nineteenth century.[25] Some use the I Ching as an object of meditation, believing that this enables one to receive insight into one's self or destiny.

This brief background of the I Ching reveals its deep spiritual and occult roots. The I Ching is clearly a tool of divination, as it is used to uncover hidden meanings in the broken and unbroken design of lines.

TEA LEAF READING

One of the classic forms of divination, reading tea leaves, is called *tasseomancy*. This term also refers to reading coffee grounds, which is often done in the area of the world where coffee is very much a part of the culture, such as in the Balkans. The tea leaf reader interprets the patterns in the leaves or grounds left in the cup after drinking.

Here again, you see the divinatory idea of finding a hidden meaning in natural things.

THE OUIJA BOARD

This is a crossover tool used in which divination is done by spirit contact, so this will be covered in the spirit-contact section.

A DANGEROUS TOOLBOX

Parents don't give young children tools such as sharp knives, scissors, or razors. In the same way, parents need to guard children from the tools of divination described in this chapter, and from books or videos that promote these things. Divination tools can cause more than physical harm because they are rooted in spiritual views opposed to God's Word, which is why children need to learn discernment in this area. Before we move on to the next chapter on magic—"real magic, not tricks"—take a look at some suggestions for teaching children about the area of divination.

BRINGING IT HOME

I am sure that you will not want to introduce your child to all of these divinatory practices, yet most older children and teens have probably been exposed to some of them already. Try to find out what your children have been exposed to and adjust your questions accordingly. (If your child has read the Harry Potter books, be aware that Harry and his friends study a divination course at Hogwarts.)

- Ask your child how he thinks a particular tool works.

- Ask: What is someone depending on if she uses tarot cards or Runes or reads tea leaves? Can the cards (or Runes, lines on the hand, or tea leaves) actually know or show what is going on in someone's life? Why or why not?

- Discuss how attempting to get information through one of these tools can take us away

from looking at God's Word or seeking him in
prayer.

- Show your child some of the biblical passages on
  divination. You can help younger children look up
  this word in a concordance and then look up the
  passages.

- A good passage to finish up with is Matthew
  10:30, in which we are told that the very hairs of
  our head are numbered. This could be a statement
  of hyperbole to emphasize God's knowledge, but
  undoubtedly God *does* know the number of hairs
  on everyone's head—all those who have ever lived,
  are living now, and will live. Talk together about
  how awesome this kind of knowledge is compared
  to the feeble efforts of man to get information
  from cards, tea leaves, lines on our hands, etc.

9

Is Magic Just in Fairy Tales?

Part One

The definition of the word "magic," as used by many ritual magicians (though usually not Wiccans or new agers) means: "Alteration of spiritual or physical essence through the conformity of will." Divine Wolf, age 15, and practitioner of ritual magic.[1]

Magic is also in Christianity too. Prayer is spellwork ... it is the use of divine energy and personal willpower to your words.[2]

*D*o you believe that casting spells and doing magic is only the stuff of fairy tales? If so, you are not alone. American culture has been bombarded with Disney cartoons and other fictional depictions of magicians in long purple robes and witches in tall black hats, so many do not realize that there are those who practice *real* magic and witchcraft.

I set up a booth at a county fair in 1996 displaying New Age and occult symbols along with the cross (the theme was "The Truth Behind the Symbols"). A young boy approached with a friend. He told me he was eleven years old and proudly showed me the figure on the necklace he was wearing. It was a serpent, the kind often seen on occult jewelry. He then told me that he had been doing magic for a while. He made it plain this was "real" magic, and that he was involved in ongoing study. Although I tried to warn him, he laughed it off and walked away when a woman called to him.

The word *magic* here does not refer to stage magic, which is merely trickery or illusion done through the skill of the magician. Nor is it fantasy magic, which includes powers made up via human imagination (such as talking to animals, being able to stretch your limbs like rubber, having X-ray vision, leaping tall buildings, spinning webs from your hands, melting objects with a glance, or other similar antics). Real magic is not considered effortless and is attempted through casting spells, complex rituals, and alleged powers of the mind and will. The goal is to bend reality to your will or to manifest a desired condition, object, or action.

Serious followers of magic have a worldview that undergirds their practice. Although some may just dabble in it, the basis for magic is not a matter of hocus-pocus or making up formulas for fun. The philosophy behind it often goes back to Gnostic views, Neoplatonism, and esoteric systems such as the Kabbalah.

Sorcery and Magic

Sorcery is a confusing word because most people in the occult today do not use it since they see it as a denigrating term. According to the Merriam-Webster dictionary, the word originally comes from a Vulgate Latin term for *chance*, and means: "the use of power gained from the assistance or control of evil spirits especially for divining."[3] This definition illustrates the ancient connection with divination as well as offering an assumption that sorcery involves contact with evil spirits.

At the initial height of Harry Potter popularity, one book that sold alongside a display of Harry Potter books in a large bookstore was *The Sorcerer's Companion: A Guide to the Magical World of Harry Potter*. This book presents the history and philosophy of various occult practices. According to this book, the term *sorcery* has had both positive and negative connotations at various points in history.[4] The authors point out that Albus Dumbledore, head of Hogwarts and mentor to Harry Potter, used the title "Grand Sorcerer" on Hogwarts letterhead.[5]

As mentioned earlier, magic is associated with "Magi" and comes from a Persian term *magus* and means: "1a: the use of means (as charms or spells) believed to have supernatural power over natural forces; 1b: magic rites or incantations; 2a: an extraordinary power or influence seemingly from a supernatural source; 2b: something that seems to cast a spell."[6]

The third definition of "magic" is given as "the art of producing illusions by sleight of hand."[7] This is a reference to stage magic, doing magic by skill and tricks, and is based on learned methods of *appearing* to do something supernatural. Tricks such as making coins disappear, pulling rabbits out of hats, sawing people in two, card tricks, and other such ruses are stage magic, and are *not* paranormal activities.

The above dictionary definition of sorcery mentions contact with spirits while the definition of *magic* does not. However, the meaning of the word magic as used today incorporates a wide range of practices, including casting spells, incantations, rituals, and contact with spirits. Occultists make distinctions in these meanings, though they do not always agree on these distinctions.

The word sorcery, as it refers to God's prohibition, will be used here interchangeably with magic, since God does not make such fine distinctions in his Word, and because the Hebrew occult terms do not always translate one-on-one with English words.

The words translated as "sorcery," "sorcerers," or "magic arts" in Galatians 5:20; Revelation 9:21; 18:23; 21:8; and 22:15 come from the Greek words *pharmakeia* for "administering a drug" and *pharmakos* for "a drug," but the context dictates that the meaning is "sorcery." Sorcery, it is believed, often involved either taking drugs or using them as part of doing magic, perhaps as a magic potion or spell, perhaps as a poison. This does not suggest that using modern drugs for healing is sorcery.

WHITE AND BLACK MAGIC: NO REAL DIFFERENCE

Many teens who practice magic or witchcraft like to say they are doing "white magic" or "white witchcraft," meaning they are using their powers for good. Using powers for a bad or selfish end, or to hurt others, is "black magic." These terms and distinctions are not used universally in the occult, though they are common. One of the most common questions I've had when speaking to youth groups, and a question I often get by e-mail, is "Is doing white magic okay since you are using magic for good?"

One of the defenses I hear from teens or tweens who play games that involve fantasy sorcery or magic is that their characters are using this power for good. This concept was popular in *The Craft*, in *Star Wars*, and in many other movies, games, and books.

Those most deeply involved in magic make no distinction between black and white magic. Even ceremonial magician and tarot-card creator Arthur Edward Waite stated that "except in a very slight, verbal and fluidic sense, no such distinction exists."[8]

Those in the occult may believe that their intention and use of power matters, but God condemns in clear language *all* such activity.

There Is "Witchcraft" and There Is "Witchcraft"

Witchcraft as a generic term refers to various practices in the occult. Used this way, it refers to the magic arts in general, and it is still used in this broad way in other cultures, sometimes being equated with sorcery. Since the twentieth century, however, the very same term (capitalized here to indicate a proper noun), *Witchcraft*, has come to be associated with a specific belief system. Witchcraft, sometimes also called Wicca, espouses a specific set of beliefs that set it apart from the generic term of *witchcraft*. This is a complex topic and will be treated only briefly here.

Though modern-day Witches and Wiccans practice occult arts, such as divination and casting spells, they are a separate group from the Magicians (those who practice Magic). Witches and Wiccans do not consider themselves sorcerers or magicians, although some of the practices of magicians described in the following section are also done by Witches and Wiccans.

Wicca is a subset of neo-paganism, an earth-based spirituality that incorporates elements of ancient pagan practices, such as polytheism and rituals centered on nature, along with revivals of Celtic and Norse paganism. Therefore, Pagans who are not part of Wicca or the modern Witchcraft religion may also use the same occult practices and have similar views of nature. Because of the lack of organizational structure, doctrine, and authority, it is not unusual to find a lot of overlap among Pagan beliefs and for practitioners to be involved in more than one area.

Wiccans are a group first started by Gerald Gardner in England in the late 1940s. Gardner, who had researched and studied occult practices for years, claimed to be reviving the "ancient religion" of witchcraft, which he called Wicca. There is no historical evidence for such a religion, though the term *witchcraft* has been used for centuries to describe the practice of various occult arts. Others who contributed to this movement were Robert Graves, whose book *The White Goddess* was published in 1948, and Alexander Sanders, who started his own Witchcraft groups. Gardner drew from the work of anthropologist Margaret Murray, whose theories about a witchcraft religion going back twenty-five thousand years have since been largely discredited.

In the 1960s, Wicca came to the United States, and this religion has grown rapidly, reaching children as well as adults. Wicca is the term most commonly used, though some dislike the term Wicca and prefer to call themselves Witches. Followers of Wicca and Witchcraft disagree on the definitions of these two terms. Witchcraft has many subset groups. Increasingly, however, the Internet is bringing Pagans and Wiccans together in a spirit of camaraderie, and perhaps to share information, political views, and environmental concerns.

Wicca is an earth-based religion, viewing the earth and nature as sacred, and usually includes worship of the Goddess and her consort, or of many gods and goddesses. Wiccans and Witches have no central authority or doctrine. Practical application of magic, rituals, and a relationship with nature are far more important. Therefore, the focus is not on doctrines but on seasonal celebrations, rituals, and cultivating a connection to the sacredness of nature and/or to the Goddess and/or the gods. The Goddess or gods might be seen as real beings, symbolic beings, as an energy or presence within all, or (in the case of the Goddess) as the earth or nature itself. Nevertheless, the Goddess or the gods are usually talked about as though they are real.

Wiccans often have an altar with symbols of their own choosing to represent the four elements of air, earth, water, and fire. A picture or drawing of a woman may represent the Goddess for those involved in Goddess worship. They typically deny the reality of absolute good or evil, instead incorporating belief in a balance between good and bad or seeing that good and bad are merely part of the whole, as reflected in the creative and destructive cycles of nature.

Their most sacred symbol is the five-pointed star (usually inscribed within a circle) called the pentacle or pentagram. The Wiccan or Witchcraft pentacle and pentagram are normally depicted with one point up and two points down. These points represent the four elements of earth, air, water, and fire, with the top point being Spirit.

Although they don't like to emphasize it, casting spells and doing magic are part of Wicca. Many Wiccans are also involved in various forms of divination such as astrology, the tarot, and numerology. Because of this occult involvement, they sometimes have contact with what they may consider to be evil spirits or forces. Wiccans have told me that they have spirits that follow them around or bother them. Sometimes, they will attempt a spell to get rid of these spirits.

One of the main attractions of Wicca is that it is experiential and open-ended, so the participants can feel they are actively involved in something of significance. There is a strong appeal of self-empowerment to young girls since the feminine powers are emphasized (the earth is viewed as feminine, and Goddess worship is an important element in Wiccan teaching). Girls who like nature and are concerned about the environment are often drawn to Wicca because of its focus on and concern for nature. Wiccan rituals and writings make them feel "connected" to nature and give teens a sense of harmony with something bigger than themselves.

Buffy's close friend Willow, on the television show *Buffy the Vampire Slayer*, is a realistic depiction of a young girl who explores Wicca and gradually becomes more confident and self-empowered as her skills grow. At one point in the storyline, Willow misuses her powers with a deadly result, but the show does not fault Wicca for this. Rather, it is presented that Willow has crossed a line and thereby brought on disaster. This is an important distinction because it reveals the rejection of objective good and evil—good and evil are weighed by intentions and results, and by the use or misuse of a neutral power, magic. This falls in line with the Wiccan or Witches' Rede: "Do no harm, do what ye will."

An Important Word about Goths, Wiccans, and Satanists

Some teens involved in Wicca may wear all-black clothes (this is not the norm for adult Wiccans, though some adults may dress this way). But keep in mind that all teens dressing in black are not necessarily Wiccan—they may consider themselves to be Goth (or Gothic). Goth is a social subculture that arose from the Punk movement in the late 1970s, which is why body piercing and hair dyeing are common to both. Some Goths are into Wicca or Eastern beliefs, though for the most part they tend to be agnostic. Goth is a culture that encompasses many beliefs and attitudes. Goths reject what they view as the shallowness and superficiality of mainstream culture, embracing as their beauty or art what society has rejected. Many artistic kids and those who feel outside of the mainstream are drawn to Goth. Those who blend Goth and Wicca may call themselves Goth Wiccans. The main thing to remember is that teens will experiment, and so they often end up combining beliefs and practices from different teachings.

Satanists, who are often confused with both Wiccans and Goths, use the pentagram, as do Wiccans, but they display it with two points up and one point down versus one point up and two points down (the normal Wiccan way). Wiccans do not generally believe in Satan, and Wiccans and Satanists dislike and often resent each other. Most contemporary Satanists do not believe in God or Satan, and instead believe that Satan is symbolic of being one's own god. They look down on Wiccans or anyone who tries to be good, often derisively calling them "white-lighters." Not all satanists use the term *satanism* for themselves. To avoid misunderstandings and inaccurate assumptions, it is critical that Christians not confuse these groups or believe that they are all one and the same.

A YOUNG MAGICIAN

After returning to the booth mentioned earlier, I learned about a teenager who was involved in white magic who wanted to know if it was okay. Since he left his name and phone number, I was able to call him. It was clear from his familiarity with certain occult books and authors that he was involved in real magic. This sixteen-year-old had a troubled history and had also been involved with drugs. He claimed to be a Christian and said he was in a Christian family. He eventually told me he would no longer practice magic, which he confirmed nearly a year later in a phone call.

This is one of the success stories. But I have also received e-mails from young teens involved with spirit contact. In the next chapter, you will see how complex and spiritually alluring this kind of magic can be.

BRINGING IT HOME

Use these ideas to reinforce the difference between fantasy and magic first introduced in chapter 3.

- Ask your child if he knows a magic trick and can show it to you. Talk about how this kind of magic is different from the magic of the occult.

- Talk to your child about this occult, or "real" magic, where one tries to gain power over the natural world. Discuss if using such power with good intentions would make it okay. Revisit Deuteronomy 18 to help your child see God's thoughts about real magic.

- Choose an account in the gospels where Jesus performs miracles of healing and shows authority over nature (see Mark 4:35–41 for the account of Jesus rebuking the sea and wind in a storm). Have your child compare Jesus' miracles (using his powers as deity) to worldly magic. Ask: When people attempt to use "real" magic to change things, how is that like trying to be God? Why is that wrong?

- If your child is older (grade eight and up), ask if she knows any Wiccans at school. Help your child understand what Wiccans believe so she will not be afraid and also not presume Wicca is harmless.

10

IS MAGIC JUST IN
FAIRY TALES?

PART TWO

*Like I said before I've been in to Magick and the Occult
sents [sic] I was 10 years old. When I was 15 years old I
become [sic] a member of an Occult Order here in C____.
The Occult Order practice [sic] many forms of Magick and
Enochian Magick was one of the forms of Magick
that it practice [sic] and I study it and Master it
with the help of the Enochian Angels.*[1]

*M*agic in Western culture has long been depicted as
fantasy or stereotyped in a cartoonish way; people deny its
existence. It is ironic, then, that our culture is dabbling in
magic through what are thought to be innocent or even
beneficial practices, such as healing with crystals, energy
healing, wearing good-luck charms, and wearing jewelry
inscribed with symbols intended to attract health, wealth,

love, or success. These are all related to magical views and techniques.

A common definition of magic is "the science and art of causing change to occur in conformity with the will."[2] Another definition is "the manipulation of subtle energies," including the energies allegedly present in many forms of Eastern healing.[3] Magic rituals are ones in which "cosmic powers, supernatural forces, deities or other non-physical beings, or the forces of nature are invoked and made subservient to the will of the magician."[4] My own definition mirrors the former: "The access, manipulation or use of an unknown and unquantifiable energy, power(s), force(s), or spirit(s) in order to bring about a desired end."

Those who engage in it see magic as neutral. In fact, true magic is thought to go beyond good or evil.

RITUAL AND CEREMONIAL MAGIC

Magicians (often referred to as *mages* in games and books) today are frequently involved in something called Ritual or Ceremonial Magic. Its practices are complex and varied and, therefore, I'll offer only enough information so you can spot certain words or concepts to know when you've come across this form of paranormal activity. It is not uncommon for some teens, especially boys, to get involved in this type of magic.

Modern-day magic has many sources: a special form of magic called Enochian Magic, the teachings of the ritual magician Aleister Crowley and others, the teachings of secret magical groups such as the Hermetic Order of the Golden Dawn and the Rosicrucians, what is purportedly ancient Hellenistic and Egyptian magic, and Kabbalah-based magic (often called the Hermetic Qabala).[5] Many of these sources are interrelated, some are distinct, but the central idea of working with energies and/or spirits in order to grow closer to or unite with the Divine[6] is the same.

The writings of Aleister Crowley (1875–1947) and the tales of his abilities and infamous persona as the "Beast" (a name he gave himself) are the inspiration for many modern-day magical practices. His phrase, which exalts man's will—"Do what thou wilt shall be the whole of the law," allegedly given him by his spirit guide and so-called Holy Guardian Angel, Aiwass—is now a motto for many satanist groups (who also may practice magic). Perhaps because of this and also due to Crowley's debauched lifestyle of drugs and degenerate sexual practices, many Christians believe Crowley was a Satanist. However, he was not. In fact, he believed that magic brings one closer to the Divine. Satanism, though it has roots back to the eighteenth century, was not practiced as an official religion until Anton La Vey founded the Church of Satan in 1966.

The belief behind many magical practices is that the Divine manifests itself downwardly from a pure plane of light, and as this expression of the Divine moves downward, the energy or light grows denser and darker until the physical plane is reached. Thus, the physical plane is the "lowest" form of energy and the furthest from the Divine. This is similar to gnostic views, and in fact, many ideas from the Gnostics are found in magic, perhaps springing from ancient magical practices at the time of gnostic teachings, or from the esoteric and gnostic Kabbalah, which gave rise to a system of magical practices outside the tradition of the Orthodox rabbinical Kabbalah. These gnostic views are in contrast to modern Paganism and Witchcraft, which revere nature and see the physical as a pure manifestation of the Divine.

Occult magic, therefore, attempts to bring into reality that which is on nonmaterial planes. This is done through rituals in which visualization,[7] altered states, the use of magical tools and magical alphabets, evocation of spirits, incantations, conjuration, and other carefully prescribed procedures are prominent. Preparation of the mind for doing magic is considered crucial. As one practitioner states, "To the magician, mind and matter are a continuity."[8] Another says, "The underlying premise of magical ritual is that if you represent a circumstance, or act out an event in your mind, it will come to pass in the world."[9] The latter statement is another way of expressing the technique of visualization.

In contrast to mischaracterizations of magic as waving a wand or saying meaningless words, practicing magic actually rests on a philosophy that true magic begins in the mind and the will of the practitioner. This is a far subtler and more complex view than most have realized, and thus is far more seductive. Although wands and other implements are used in magic, these are seen as mere tools, or even props, which help the magician act out the power *already* within him.

Ritual magic consists of complicated rituals and ceremonies that become theoretically more powerful and effective as the practitioner increases in skill and experience. Magicians who believe they are practicing "high" magic, a more complex form of the magical arts, believe that not only are they improving themselves, but also that they are helping humanity evolve. One practitioner, speaking of all people, states, "We are in the process of becoming *more than human*, of being better than we currently are."[10]

Two terms should be understood, though sometimes they are used interchangeably: *invocation* and *evocation*. Invocation is calling for aid from spirits, elemental forces (of nature), gods, goddesses, spirit guides, angels, or some kind of energy or force. This term is also used by some to mean calling up these spirits or gods into one's self.

Evocation is calling up or summoning a spirit, elemental force, god, goddess, or energy for communication and/or aid in doing magic, i.e., doing the magician's bidding. Magicians believe they are contacting an entity in the astral plane, a nonmaterial plane of reality beyond the physical. They do not necessarily believe this entity will appear on the physical plane, though it might have a physical appearance; it is enough to evoke the entity *astrally* (visible only in the astral plane by someone who is in an altered state).

Invocation is sometimes seen as a request, while evocation is considered a command and is associated more with magical rituals than invocation. Sometimes the distinction claimed between the two is that evocation is used to manifest the appearance of a spirit being, while invocation is used to call the spirit or entity into one's self. One constant in the occult is there is *no* constant in what some occult terms mean or how they are applied!

Before a ritual, the magician must purify himself or herself and don special clothes or a magical robe. The magician may visualize a white light infusing the area where he or she will cast a protective circle. After this, various techniques and rituals are followed, according to the tradition the magician is following.

What will surprise many Christians is that many of the incantations recited in these forms of magic involve saying various biblical names of God.[11] Magicians believe such names have a power they can access through the rituals. Most magicians also believe that Solomon, Moses, and Jesus were advanced practitioners of magic. There is even such a thing as "Solomon's seal" used in magic. Some magicians believe that an angel gave Solomon a magic ring that enabled Solomon to control various spirits.[12]

Magicians usually keep a record of their rituals and the results in a magical diary. (Witches and Wiccans do this with spells and rituals in the *Book of Shadows*.)

RUNES AND SIGILS: MAGIC SYMBOLS

Runes, symbols associated with Norse paganism, are used for both divination (see chapter 8) and for magic. Each rune is thought to be "the occult name and sigil of one of the most fundamental forces of existence."[13] A sigil is a symbol believed to contain the essence and power of a spirit or deity. The word comes from the Latin *sigillum*, meaning "seal," and sometimes the word *seal* is used to refer to a sigil. Sigils may be in the form of "geometric shapes, astrological signs, alchemical symbols, crosses," and other signs.[14]

A book for teens advises them on how to make their own sigils for "the pursuit of angel magic." The author counsels her readers, "Sigils are virtually mistake-proof. You draw it, you empower it, and that's all there is."[15] In her discussion of angels and angel magic, the author, who also wrote *Teen Witch*, blatantly denies the existence of fallen or evil angels.[16]

Runes are seen as a type of sigil when used in magic. They "form the magical language of the northern gods and express the forces upon which those gods are named; manipulating them gives direct control over the actions not only of the deities, but also of the spirits and lesser entities of Norse mythology."[17] This is the magical view that one can learn to control the spirit world through various occult tools, such as using the supernatural power of runes. Rune magic is thought to be the most dangerous, according to one practitioner, and can bring on violence.[18]

Amulets and Talismans

Amulets are objects, drawings, or symbols that are believed to have powers of protection against evil, disease, and other harm. The most familiar ones are good-luck charms, such as a rabbit's foot, four-leaf clover, or a lucky penny (these can also be seen as talismans). Someone who practices magic, however, might imbue an object intended to be an amulet with protective power through some kind of meditation, ritual, or spell.

Crystals, typically quartz, semiprecious, or precious stones, are believed to contain and emit certain kinds of energy or vibrations that can be used for healing, protection, mental clarity, to enhance love, or to attract success and prosperity. The owner will wear the crystal, carry it, or place it somewhere in the home. When I received a large crystal from a grateful astrology client, I was instructed to place it in a glass of salted water for twenty-four hours to cleanse it, then leave it near a window for a while in the sun, and finally meditate on it in order to charge it or program it with my "energy." Not surprisingly, crystals are often used as amulets (as well as healing agents).

Amulets are usually worn as jewelry or carried in a pouch tied around the neck. An amulet might also be a prayer, magical phrase, or a secret symbol written on paper or inscribed on an object. This is then carried around the neck, kept in a pouch or box, or placed above a doorway or bed. A popular amulet is the *ankh*, a symbol from ancient Egypt. This is a cross topped by a loop, and represents immortality as well as the combination of a male and female symbol (the cross is male and the loop is female). Wearing an ankh is widespread in both the New Age movement and the occult, particularly with those involved in either Egyptian magic or the vampire subculture.

Another revived ancient Egyptian symbol and talisman is the Eye of Horus, which can be seen on T-shirts and jewelry. A red string worn around the wrist to protect against the "evil eye" or negative energies is becoming better known through the popularized Kabbalah.

Other familiar amulets are horseshoes hung above doorways and strings of garlic worn or displayed supposedly to protect against vampires. Many semiprecious stones, such as the amethyst, are thought to have protective powers. Amulets vary according to different cultural beliefs and customs.[19] Some Runes are used as amulets.

A *talisman*, by contrast, is an object, drawing, or symbol believed to have supernatural powers that can be passed on to the person who possesses it. The object is "endowed with paranormal power by the forces of nature, by God or the gods or by being made in a ritualistic way."[20] A talisman can be used to attract success, money, good health, love, or power, or to confer health, clarity of thought, or other desired attributes. This is precisely the idea behind common good-luck charms, such as four-leaf clovers or the rabbit's foot—that these objects will actually draw fortune to the owner or in some way bring protective power from the forces or spirits in charge.

Talismans are active, whereas amulets are passive and usually used to protect or ward off evil. Some talismans are used for curing illness. The philosopher's stone (called a sorcerer's stone in Harry Potter books published in the United States) was considered a talisman in alchemy, thought to be able to confer immortality.[21] In the practice of Feng Shui, the Chinese characters for success, fortune, or health are inscribed on doors or papers hung in various parts of a house in order to attract those things.

Amulets and talismans reveal the occult belief that objects or writing can actually contain power. Although the use of these objects in a magical ritual would most likely engage the demonic world, the objects themselves do not contain power. To believe so is an occult world-view. In fact, *animism,* a view found in many pagan cultures, is the belief that objects can be inhabited by spirits.

CASTING SPELLS

What is a spell? A look at three definitions will be helpful. One simple definition is: "A spell is a procedure to follow to reach a desired end."[22] Another witch states, "A spell is a spoken or written formula that, in an act of magic, is intended to cause or influence a particular course of events."[23] The Farrars, a couple prominent in the Witchcraft community in England and influential in the United States, put it this way, "A spell is a ritual for raising psychic power and directing it to a specific and practical purpose" and is "fueled by vivid imagination and concentrated willpower."[24] Older terms for spells include "enchantment" and "bewitching." Spells can be done for good or for harm, but don't forget that magic is seen as "a neutral force that in itself is neither good nor evil."[25]

The most likely practitioners of spells are followers of Witchcraft or Wicca, though anyone can do spells. Spells involve rituals, incantations, and various tools and vary widely in the way they are done. Spells can be cast alone or with a group. Candle magic, burning various colors of candles to effect a specific outcome, has attracted many young girls, and books and other information on this popular practice have increased.

Many witches compare casting spells to prayer. In their view, it is the same thing because one is calling on a power for assistance. This power may come from nature, spirits of nature, deities, "divinity," the Goddess, or Spirit,[26] and may be seen as supernatural or natural. Spells also may call for going into an altered state, "raising energy," belief in the power of being able to do the spell, and the strength of one's will. ("Raising energy" is being empowered by a natural or supernatural force in order to cast the spell and can be done through visualization of the goal, chanting, moving around a circle, or some other means.)

Back in the 1980s, when I was involved in ongoing protests against the building of a particular road through a park, I joined a group of people at one protest site who were forming a circle. We were told how to move in the circle and then to move faster and faster. We were told we were "raising energy." My memory is sketchy, but I believe a meditation followed the spirited dancing. Later, some of us were given objects to bury at various locations where the road was planned—these objects supposedly were imbued with a power or spell to stop the road. Not surprisingly, the people orchestrating these events were involved in Wicca or Witchcraft. (The road was not built, but this undoubtedly was due to political and civic action that was also taking place against the road.)

The mind and its power are essential ingredients in spell working; thus, techniques such as visualization and meditation are important. Deities or spirits may also be called on to accomplish a spell.

The Hebrew *chabar* is from a root word for *join* or *unite* and can mean "to tie a magic knot" or "to charm."[27] This term is found in Deuteronomy 18:11 and is usually translated in this verse as "one who casts a spell" or "a charmer." In light of the meaning about tying a magic knot, it is interesting to note that tying knots is a part of folk magic and witchcraft around the world. It is believed that power is bound and released by the tying and untying of the knot, and such knots are used to work spells. In this passage God strongly condemns any spell casting or charming.

MAGIC AS SELF-EMPOWERMENT

Many young people are attracted to magic because it is presented as a way to be self-empowered. Practicing magic can seem like a self-improvement course: "The magician's willpower and concentration are vigorously exercised. His ability to visualize is improved. His understanding of the universe becomes a little deeper, as does his understanding of himself."[28]

Magician Donald Tyson says that magic "opens a new awareness of the world where dreams can happen, and where human actions do have meaning. It opens on hope and purpose" and magic ritual can change one on several levels, "physical, emotional, mental, and spiritual."[29]

One book states that those who understand and know how to use the energies of magic are taking "a big bite of the apple from the biblical Tree of Wisdom."[30] This is why magic often attracts intelligent kids who are not finding an outlet in other ways, or who are socially immature or awkward. Magic makes them feel special, clever, powerful, and superior to others.

It is interesting that Galatians 5:20 lists sorcery as a sin of the flesh. Why would this be? Sorcery appeals to the senses and to one's pride. It is based on a belief that one can control certain powers and spirit beings like angels, and that one can reach God through one's own efforts. This attitude negates the necessity for a Savior and the great price paid on the cross by Jesus for sin.

MAGIC ALL AROUND US

You may be thinking that magic is strange or alien or rare. Quite the opposite is true. Perhaps you've seen jewelry inscribed with the Chinese characters for fortune, health, prosperity, and long life. Maybe you know someone who knocks on wood after certain statements. These fall in with what is called magical thinking—an acceptance of the belief that an object or symbol can bring protection or good fortune.

Even Christians can fall into this by thinking that anointing their home with oil can keep demons out. The oil itself has no power at all—all that is needed is to pray and ask God for protection. The oil can be used as a symbol of God's protection or presence if so desired, but the oil itself has no special powers.

People have always been impressed by what seems to be supernatural power, whether it is or isn't. Acts talks about Simon the sorcerer of Samaria who was "astonishing" the people so much, that they called him "the Great Power of God" (Acts 8:9–10). In denouncing the wickedness of Babylon, God tells them that though their "many sorceries" may bring them profit and even cause "trembling," none of their skills, wealth, or powers will save them (Isaiah 47:12).

But those who practice magic are always shown to be against God's truth. Former practitioners of the magic arts burned their books when they turned to Christ (see Acts 19:18–19). In Paul's first missionary journey, Paul and Barnabas had traveled to give the gospel to the proconsul in Cyprus, but Elymas the magician tried to *"turn the proconsul away from the faith"* (Acts 13:8). Pharaoh's magicians, who duplicated Moses' act of turning water into blood and bringing on hordes of frogs into the land by their "secret arts" (Exodus 7:22; 8:7), are condemned by the Lord in the

New Testament and compared to men who "oppose the truth" (2 Timothy 3:8). There is clearly no compatibility between magic and serving God.

Before the discussion in the next chapter on specific games that use ideas and terms from magic, it would be good to help your child understand magical thinking and why it is unbiblical.

Bringing It Home

If you have any good-luck charms around, use these as an object lesson and then get rid of them!

- Ask your child if he knows what luck is. Surely your child has heard or even used the term *Good luck*. Explain that luck is belief in an object being able to protect or bring good things. Ask your child if an object can do this.

- Now ask your child how much power God has. Explain omnipotence if your child does not know that term. Which is better, to think an object can help us or to pray to God for help? Who has more power?

- If your child knows anyone who does magic or spells in school, or if your child has seen movies or TV shows about this, your child might wonder if someone can cast a spell to harm her. This is something to discuss and it is essential to explain that no one has this kind of power. Those in the occult are being used by Satan—they are *used* by occult power; they don't control it.

- Have your child read the account in Exodus
  7:8–13, where Pharaoh's magicians turn their
  staffs into serpents, which are then eaten by
  Aaron's staff, which had miraculously become a
  serpent. Then go to Exodus 8:18, where the magicians are unable to duplicate the plague of gnats,
  even though they previously were able to do what
  appeared to be supernatural feats. Ask your child
  what the magicians say in the next verse (19) and
  start a discussion on this.

11

MAGIC AS A GAME

*Some Witches or ceremonial workers give their tools a
magickal "name". (This practice has become a common
reference in many role-playing games and fantasy novels.)*[1]

*My first wife was a Wiccan. And she told me that D&D got
her interested in witchcraft.*[2]

*T*he computer-savvy kids of today can, with one or two
clicks, visit any of the thousands of kid-friendly sites offering games that incorporate occult magic concepts, or sites
with serious occult information.

If your child plays video or online games, ask questions
about the characters, terms used, and the actions. If anything looks like magic or divination, check it out. Video

games also use fantasy, and fantasy is normal and healthy if not tainted by occult concepts. However, in many games, the characters must use sorcery or magic to win.

New games are released all the time, so we can't cover them all here. However, the principles in examining and responding to the specific games discussed in this chapter can be applied to any video or card game.

DUNGEONS & DRAGONS

Dungeons & Dragons (D&D) is a complex FRPG (Fantasy Role Playing Game) strategy game, now also played on the Internet and in video or computer games. To begin, players choose a character to role-play, and each character can have different abilities, traits, and levels of points. The game is supervised and directed by an experienced player known as the Dungeon Master. Characters with paranormal powers often have a higher status than other characters.

In Advanced Dungeons & Dragons (AD&D), characters with magical powers, such as wizards, "may well be the most important character class in the AD&D game."[3] Players are continually coming up with new strategies for their characters, and the game has seemingly endless options to offer in character traits, histories, and talents. Within D&D lies a whole fantasy world.

For a period of time I subscribed to *Dragon Magazine*, a periodical for players of D&D. Every issue had at least one article on spells, mages (magicians), and other characters who had supernormal powers. One issue featured "Wizards of Dusk & Gloom" and "A Little Bit of Magic," articles that gave information and pointers on magical practices to players of the game. "Wizards of Dusk & Gloom" introduced "shadow mages" who "dabble in unwholesome magic" and whose spells have "a tendency toward the sinister."[4]

The shadow mages include a "shadow caller," "shadow seeker," and "shadow hunter." The article bluntly stated that the "shadow caller's practice of magic is frequently violent, ritualistic, and dramatic."[5] Shadow seekers tend toward "bouts of melancholy" and shadow hunters use their magic for "theft or assassination."[6] Other unsavory traits abound, including many references to monsters, paranormal powers, and death.

Another issue contained articles titled "Grim Callings," "Legacy of Decay," "101 Hauntings," "Mather's Blood," and "Bazaar of the Bizarre."[7] Some of the terms used in relation to the characters or their powers include *necromancy, divination, summoning spirits, re-animation of the dead, casting spells, enchantment, magical protections, wizard, contact the dead, spectral, demonic, neutral evil, chaotic evil, conjure,* and more.

One article offers various "adventure starters" that can be introduced into any game. Two of the categories for these "adventures" are "Murder & Mayhem" and "Cruelty and Revenge." Almost all of them are grim. Consider this one: A young woman who is mentally ill dies and "her spirit is transferred to a doll. By commanding the child who owns the doll, she manages to orchestrate the deaths of her family members whom she saw as cruel and spiteful."[8] Accompanying these articles are illustrations of morbid-looking and repulsive characters.

Several D&D books that give information and advice on the magical powers used in the game are offered as options to help players handle their characters more skillfully. Under a section titled "The Cost of Magic," one book states, "Wizards may have to make terrible pacts with dark powers for the knowledge they seek, priests may have to sacrifice something dear to them to invoke their deity's favor, or the spellcaster may pay an immediate price in terms of fatigue, illness, or even a loss of sanity."[9]

Spells are grouped into various categories, such as *Abjuration, Alteration, Conjuration/Summoning, Enchantment/Charm, Divinations, Illusion/Phantasm, Invocation/Evocation, Necromancy, and Universal Magic.*[10] The special spells and powers available to various game characters are described at length, often in colorful detail.

In addition, bits of occult or pagan philosophy are scattered throughout the books, such as the statement that "all forms of life contain a spark of magical energy, sharing a mystical life force that a wizard can use to power his spells."[11]

A disturbing section describes various forms of insanity that may afflict a character in the game. Some of these are actual forms of mental disturbance such as *catatonia* and *schizophrenia*, and each is vividly described. One is a mania that causes the afflicted to "turn on and kill people close to him," while another is a madness whereby the character is controlled by an "invasive persona" that "wants nothing more than to kill until it is sated."[12]

Although D&D is only a game and is not the actual practice of an occult art, the game itself contains many aspects that relate to occult practices, even using the same terms. Dark imagery and violence intensify as the player becomes more advanced, at the very least desensitizing the player to the bizarre, deviant, and morbid. This is clearly not wholesome; the player is exposing his or her mind to concepts and terms that are at odds with biblical teaching and with healthy mental and emotional development.

MAGIC: THE GATHERING

A card game created in 1993, Magic: The Gathering (MtG), spread from coast to coast, selling a billion cards within eighteen months. Its Oregon makers, Wizards of the Coast, described this game as a fantasy trading card game. The creator is mathematician and veteran Dungeons & Dragons player Richard Garfield.[13]

The cards are linked to one of five kinds of magic: red, blue, green, white, or black. The players assume the roles of wizards or mages, using the cards to defeat their opponents in the game. The cards "represent the lands, creatures, spells, and artifacts" for each player.[14] The term *mana* is used to mean the "magical energy used for casting spells and activating special powers."[15] This term, *mana*, was also used in the movie *The Craft* to refer to a magical force or power, and it crops up in games with magical themes. The use of this word in magic is disputed. It may derive from a Norse mythological concept of mana as a vital life essence, or from Polynesian religious concepts of power held by one in authority. As used today in games that feature magic, mana seems to be the equivalent of what in many cultures is believed to be a life essence, energy, or force that can be harnessed and used for healing or supernatural magic. This concept is discussed at more length in chapter 15.

Like Dungeons & Dragons, MtG is a challenging game that calls for intricate strategy and shrewd plays. However, that strategy is worked out within the context of dark images and occult terms. Many cards portray frightening and repellent creatures. Skeletons, blood, and images of death are common. There's the Bone Shaman, the Necrite (depicted licking blood off a dagger), Prodigal Sorcerer, Dark Ritual, Sadistic Glee, Torture, Sorceress Queen, Soul Drinker, Fallen Angel, Endless Scream, and others. One card showing several skeletons and called The Kjeldoran

Dead has this quote: *"'They shall kill those whom once they loved.' C Lim-Dul, the Necromancer."* Necromancy is communication with the dead through supernatural and/or occult techniques.

Parents should consider the possible results of exposure to these images and terms:

- Desensitization to what is macabre, evil, or repulsive

- Desensitization to sorcery and occult terms

- Familiarity with occult terms and concepts

- Development of a taste for the bizarre

Some kids will point out that many of these Magic cards are "good" cards and depict nature or even angels. They will say that the ugly cards are the "black" cards. However, pleasant images on many cards do not negate the fact that the players are still in the role of a magician playing with cards that represent casting spells and doing magic. Second, one of the most chilling cards I've seen is actually a white card, supposedly a "good" card. It portrays a sorceress, Justina, who imbues her weapon with her life force in order to slay a monster, "thus fulfilling the prophecy that in your savior will you find salvation." This is a clear counterfeit to Jesus and is typical of occult language that attacks Christ under the guise of something presented as spiritual or benevolent.

A comic book based around this game features a young man who, in the course of his adventures, meets a mystical woman in a forest, Kristina of the Woods. Kristina takes the hero, Jared, under her wing and teaches him about magic. In her discourse, she explains that magic "can take your imaginings, Jared, and make them real."[16] Kristina goes on to inform him that "white, like all magic, is in itself neither good nor evil."[17] It is interesting but also distressing to see the actual occult philosophy about magic in a comic book based on a card game!

YU-GI-OH

Yu-Gi-Oh, originally a comic created in Japan in 1996 by Kazuki Takahashi, was about a boy, Yugi, playing a card game called "Dueling Monsters" (originally called "Magic & Wizards") and his adventures. This story gave birth to a card game that has spawned movies, a TV cartoon, and video games. The general story tells of Yugi becoming inhabited by a five-thousand-year-old pharaoh, Yama Yugi, as they try to solve the mystery of an ancient puzzle. Another site suggests that Yugi is taken over by "dark Yugi" when he needs to work on the puzzle.[18] I imagine few parents are aware of this story background. One of the Game Boy adaptations of this game is enthusiastically described as "based on the Shadow Game—a mystic ritual involving actual monsters and spells that was performed in ancient Egypt 5,000 years ago."[19]

Like other similar card games, new series of decks are coming out all the time, with titles like "Dark Revelation," "Blaze of Destruction," "Magician's Force," and "Zombie Madness."[20] The Yugi Starter Deck has cards named Dark Magician, Summoned Skull, Book of Secret Arts, Sorcerer of the Doomed, and Ultimate Offering.[21] The Magician's Force series contains cards such as Skilled White Magician, Skilled Dark Magician, Apprentice Magician, Amazoness Spellcaster, Hidden Book of Spell, Double Spell, and others.[22] A series called "Ancient Sanctuary" has cards such as Talisman of Spell Sealing, Spirit Caller, Grave Protector, and

Dark Magic Attack.[23] There are even cards called "ritual magic cards."

One commentator on the movie version of this game states, "Powers are divined from ancient artifacts, unearthed spirits, spells chanted in an eerie foreign tongue ... Yugi derives energy and card-playing prowess from a spirit called Pharaoh that inhabits the medallion he wears around his neck. During duels, Yugi seems 'possessed' by the spirit which deepens his voice and 'shadows' him during card play."[24]

Needless to say, this subject matter is disturbing and dark.

THE VAMPIRE GAMES

Role-playing games based on the world of vampires have recently shown an increase in popularity both on the Internet and off. One of the more unique (and potentially troubling) trends is vampire Live Action Role Playing Games (LARPGs), such as Vampire: The Masquerade, Vampire: The Requiem, and others. (Some of these are also available as computer or video games.) The books for these games describe dark and bizarre situations involving the drinking of blood and murder. The term *feeding*, meaning to suck the blood of another human, is used throughout, and the vampires are described as predators and killing machines who struggle constantly with their baser instincts. If they lose this struggle, they can descend into an almost insane frenzy in their hunt for blood.

Vampire powers that might be assigned to some characters include telepathy, psychic projection, psychometry, and possession of another's body. Many characters have occult abilities, and supernormal power and strength is a key element of the fantasy. Ritual Magician Crowley's famous motto, "Do what thou wilt shall be the whole of the law," is even quoted in one game book in describing a particular group of vampires who believe they are incarnated demons.[25]

The game is supposed to be played out in a controlled environment; hence its origins in clubs set aside for that purpose. The books state the purpose is merely for entertainment, and suggestions in the books can sound like stage directions for a play. However, the intrigue around vampirism has attracted many who act out the game in the streets or wherever players might gather. While most players stick to the game format, some take the fantasy into reality and believe they are vampires. These players imitate the vampire role by wearing artificial fangs, or sometimes even have their incisors sharpened to resemble fangs.

It is not unheard of to find teens who succumb to the vampire fantasy by actually practicing blood drinking with others. I first heard of this in the schools when some teens in a youth group asked me about it back in 1996. I receive many e-mails from those who identify with the vampire persona, ranging from those who play the game to those who believe they have become a true vampire and are not human.

WORLD OF WARCRAFT

Another role-playing game—this one, a computer game—is World of Warcraft, which, by its title, seems to be simply a war game. On closer inspection, however, it turns out to be a mélange of war strategy, occult concepts, and New Age spirituality. It has four main "races" of beings: humans, "one of the youngest races of the world"; Orcs, who were once part of a "noble, Shamanistic society"; Night Elves, who misused magic; and Undead Scourge, who consist of "thousands of walking corpses, disembodied spirits, damned mortal men, and insidious extra-dimensional entities."[26] The Legendary Heroes possess "different attributes from one another including unique abilities and spells."[27] Each race has its own heroes and particular powers.

The humans are aided by the "Holy Light," and include characters such as Blood Mage and Archmage, and Priest and Sorceress. The latter can aid warriors with "specialized conjurings and magical effects."[28] One of the powers of the Archmage is his ability to summon water elementals. This is rather unsettling considering that, in actual occult magic, creatures or powers called "elementals" are summoned.

The Orcs seem to be equated with the Native Americans since terms such as *spirit lodge* and *totem* are used. Orc characters include Shaman, Spirit Walker, and Witch Doctor. One of the Orc heroes is a Far Seer, who is "tied to the elements of the earth and sky" and can foretell the future.[29] The Shaman, not surprisingly, draws power from the natural world and the elements.

Many contemporary games incorporate power in the form of magic and spells. Sheer power has become central to stories and games today, replacing former qualities such as moral fiber, integrity, and honesty.

LAMAR'S STORY

Lamar, now in his thirties, was once involved with many games mentioned here. He started off with D&D in the fourth grade, later becoming involved with other role-playing games and games such as Magic: The Gathering. He offers this testimony:

> I was a hardcore gamer throughout high school. I researched the occult and witchcraft to make my games better, and they were. Everyone wanted to be in my games. I devoted most of my free time to D&D for years.
>
> Once I graduated I got married and didn't play as much any more. But that didn't last more than a couple of years. Then I was back to it. I worked three and four days a week (12 hour shifts), and then spent 2–3 days working on my game.
>
> I soon was introduced to other role-playing games like Vampire: The Masquerade, and Champions: The Super-Hero Role Playing Game, and Top Secret (espionage). I ran those as well.
>
> Finally, my wife talked me into stopping the RPGs. I did so reluctantly, but soon found a new fix in Magic: The Gathering. In the space of two or three months, I had sunk close to four hundred dollars into cards, not to mention the decks and cards that I stole, which were probably worth twice that.[30]

Lamar started young but continued playing these games into adulthood, even after marriage. Note that he researched the occult to make his D&D games better. Thankfully, Lamar finally got rid of his games through the help of his wife and the Lord, and now recognizes the danger of these games.

WHAT'S IN A GAME?

It is important not to equate a game with practicing the occult. This only causes adults to lose credibility in the eyes of their children because even kids recognize the difference. Acknowledge to your children that playing a strategy game is not the same as engaging in an occult practice. Many bright kids are attracted to the strategy games of Magic: The Gathering, D&D, Yu-Gi-Oh, World of Warcraft, and others. These kinds of games require complex planning and concentration. Many kids who play these games are not interested in real spells or magic and seem, outwardly at least, unaffected by such concepts. Two things to keep in mind, however, are that no one can tell who will be affected by exposure to these games, and the effects taking place are not necessarily visible.

It is valuable to distinguish between the productive and healthy use of fantasy and the unhealthy use of fantasy. Fantasy and imagination play a crucial role, allowing us to create, to appreciate beauty, and to be entertained. But just as any human trait or talent, fantasy and imagination can be misused. Instead of images evoking death and darkness, consider God's words in Philippians 4:8 that instruct believers to dwell on what is true, honorable, pure, and lovely.

Before going where angels tread in the next chapter, here are some suggestions for teaching your child ways to deal with games that include occult concepts.

BRINGING IT HOME

Responding to your child's objections to any prohibition on these games is covered in a later chapter. The points below are designed to help children think through what was discussed in this chapter regarding games that use occult terms or concepts so that they can see why these games are undesirable.

- Ask your child to think of something ugly or gross, like eggs with cotton candy, or milk mixed with bugs. How does your child feel when thinking about this? Would he want to see this image all the time? Have your child compare this image with what is often found in games that is similarly ugly or gross. Use this as a starting point to talk about good choices regarding games.

- Ask: How do you think God sees things like those in the game that are ugly or gross? Should we be involved in things that promote practices that God finds ugly and sinful?

- Ask your child if she can unwatch a television show, unsee a picture, or unread a book. Of course, this isn't possible. Once an image is in the mind, it is hard to get it out. Ask: If God has forgiven us through Christ, even though sin is so repellent to him, how should we respond when choosing what to put in our minds? How should we use the imagination that God has given us?

12

ANGELS OF LIGHT: DECEPTION FROM BEYOND

PART ONE

I respect greatly Christ etc., but Dogmas are killing everyone and destroying the universe. If we simply focused on the 7 Spiritual Laws, Angels and direct God communications, all in the world would be well.[1]

Angels create bridges between various religions.[2]

Angels, you will discover, can be reached through meditation, will assist you in connecting with your higher self, bring important messages and advice to you, and yes, even help you work through reincarnation memories.[3]

Touched By An Angel was one of the most popular television shows of the 1990s. In the past few years, interest in angels, spirits, and contacting the dead has been steadily growing.[4] Angels and contacting spirits or the dead often fascinate non-Christians because they see this as spiritual activity, and they feel they are connecting with something sacred and wise.

Many movies and television shows depict angels and mediums, those who contact the dead. *The Sixth Sense*, a movie about a young boy who could see and hear from dead people, was a big hit, and was only one of several movies with themes related to after-death communication. Other noted movies on after-death communication include: *The Others, Beneath the Surface, Dragonfly,* and *White Noise,* the latter proposing that some hear messages from the dead through the static of white noise.

Popular medium John Edward went from the Sci-Fi channel with his show, *Crossing Over*, to nation-wide syndication. The television show *Medium* was a surprise sleeper hit on NBC, and CBS's *The Ghost Whisperer* is yet another show on this topic, featuring a young woman who communicates with the recently departed to help them resolve issues with those still living or make peace so they can "cross over." The Web site for this show has a link to a blog, placed on the CBS site, run by medium James Van Praagh, who is coproducer of the series.[5] And, of course, the Ouija board is still with us.

WHO ARE THE SPIRITS?

Since many refer to the dead as "spirits," there is a lot of misunderstanding on this subject. "Spirit contact" is the broad term covering contact with disembodied beings, whether one believes them to be angels, dead people, spirit guides, spiritual masters, aliens, ascended masters, beings on other planes or in other dimensions, or other types of discarnate entities. Methods of contact may include a séance, messages received through a medium, channeling, automatic writing, the Ouija board, or visions or dreams.

Dead people are usually referred to by mediums and Spiritualists as "spirits," but dead people are *not* spirits. The only spirit creatures, according to the Bible, are angels. Although humans have spirits (or souls, depending on whether or not one believes "soul" and "spirit" to be the same thing), we are not spirit beings. A dead person is not an angel nor is a dead person *ever* an angel or a spirit being. Angels, the true spirit beings, and humans, are two different categories of creation.

WHO CONTACTS SPIRITS?

Mediums, channelers, and psychics are involved either knowingly or unknowingly in spirit contact. Not all psychics are mediums, but all mediums are psychics. Mediums contact beings they believe to be dead (usually recently dead) by allowing a spirit to speak through them or by passing on messages from the dead. These readings are done at séances, privately, or in public settings.

Séances are done with a group of people, usually in a dimly lit room. The medium calls for protection by asking to be surrounded by white light or protective spirits; the medium summons spirits interested in contact, or tries to contact the spirit of a departed loved one. Technically speaking, even two people trying to contact a dead person, perhaps through a Ouija board, are also conducting a séance.

Private readings are done between the medium, channeler or psychic and the individual seeking contact. Public readings are often done on television shows, such as *Crossing Over* with John Edward, who claims to receive messages from the dead relatives of those in the audience. Other popular mediums in the U.S. are Sylvia Browne and James Van Praagh.

Channelers usually contact spirit beings other than the recently dead—including angels, aliens, advanced spiritual beings, and enlightened beings. They may do this by allowing the spirit to speak through them, or they may simply pass on a message given to them. These messages are typically targeted not for an individual, but for the group that is present at the channeling, or sometimes even for *all* people. These messages received by channelers often have strong spiritual overtones and typically exhort people to be more concerned for the environment, to avoid war, to be more loving and tolerant, and not to take any "religious book" too seriously or think that there is just one true religion. J. Z. Knight claims to channel Ramptha, who asserts that he is a thirty-five-thousand-year-old warrior. Lazaris is an entity channeled by Jach Pursel. Jane Roberts claimed to receive messages from an entity calling himself "Seth," who first contacted her via a Ouija board. The messages from Seth are chronicled in the book *Seth Speaks* and other books.

Ruth Montgomery, alluded to in the section on automatic writing, wrote several books of teachings channeled from the "guides" who advised her. The very popular and influential *A Course in Miracles* was channeled by Helen Schucman, an atheist, who said that the spirit speaking to her was Jesus Christ. This resulted in a thick book, often simply referred to as *The Course,* which was used by groups across the country in the 1970s and 1980s as a spiritual guide. Many followers of this book became deeply involved in the New Age. One of those followers is Marianne Williamson, who has written best sellers such as *A Return to Love,* which was itself based on *A Course in Miracles.*

Psychics may use spirit guides, angels, or the supposed spirits of deceased teachers or gurus as a way to help them do their readings, though this is not always the case. Sometimes psychics may be unaware of the help they are getting from spirits.

In addition to the psychics and mediums, Spiritualists contact the dead as part of their religious beliefs. *Spiritualism* is a term referring to the practice of contacting the dead, but it is also a religion. Spiritualist churches, many of which belong to the National Spiritualist Association of Churches in the United States, are popular with mediums and psychics.

Spirit guides are considered to be wise souls who have passed on from life here on Earth and have since dedicated themselves to helping those still alive. Children are sometimes unwittingly introduced to spirit guides. Visualization exercises have been (and may still be) offered, even at the elementary level. In some of these exercises, the children are introduced to a "special friend." They are told they can ask or tell anything to this special friend, even things they might have a hard time telling their parents. They're also told that this friend can visit them anytime. Though the visualization technique may seem simply like a useful tool for helping children deal with life, this is essentially an introduction to a spirit guide. A spirit guide always appears wise and benevolent but is actually a demon. Spirit guides are used in occult and New Age practices, and people not even seeking such guides have been contacted by them when dabbling in the occult.

The Messages from Beyond

One thing all these spirits have in common is that they give messages often contradictory to the Bible and to Christian doctrine. The messages are sometimes not only contradictory but blatantly hostile to Christ or Christianity, or promote ideas contrary to Christianity. The messages also often deny the reality of evil.

A Course in Miracles talks about God, Jesus, and the Holy Spirit, but with a twist. For example, it claims that the body was not made by God, but is a result of wrong perception that keeps us in the illusion of separation from God.[6] There is no need for guilt, because there is no sin; sin is illusory.[7] Although mankind makes mistakes, the perception of sin is an error to be corrected.[8] The Atonement is redefined as a way to cancel errors man could not correct, and when one is "restored" to his original state of realizing his guiltlessness, he attains heaven and becomes part of this Atonement.[9] Marianne Williamson, in her book based on *The Course*, writes that Christ is "a psychological term" that "refers to the common thread of divine love that is the core and essence of every human mind."[10]

In one of the *Seth* books, the channeled entity Seth explains that man was born in a state of grace, and that it is impossible for man to leave it.[11] A common teaching from beyond, whether from the dead, from a supposed "Jesus" or "God," or from angels or aliens, is that since man comes from God and is part of God, man is inherently good, having a divine inner nature.[12]

I attended several Spiritualist church services during college because one friend was doing a project on Spiritualism, and since she did not want to go alone, a group of us went with her. The ministers of these churches are mediums. At one particular Spiritualist gathering, we wrote questions to deceased relatives or friends and dropped them in a box. I wrote a question to my paternal grandfather, who had died suddenly about two years earlier, and who had died an atheist. My written question was asking if he was happy where he was.

During the service, the minister briefly explained that his "control," the spirit who spoke through him and would give messages from the dead, would take over. He went into a trance, and the control spoke in a strangely different voice from that of the minister. Someone tied a heavy black cloth around the medium's eyes, and he drew questions from the box (supposedly reading them psychically since he could not see). He chose my question, and gave the answer that yes, my grandfather was very happy and at peace where he was. I was not a believer then and was satisfied with the answer.

The movie *Ghostbusters* comically portrayed a group of people who "chased" ghosts out of haunted places, but there are real ghostbusters. These mediums or psychics visit alleged haunted houses or other places in order to converse with the departed spirit and find out what is keeping the deceased from moving on. At the organization where I first studied astrology and psychic development, mediums hired themselves out to people who wanted help to remove a presence or haunting from their home. These mediums claimed they could communicate with these troubled "ghosts" in order to encourage these spirits of the dead to leave the earthly plane.

Another common message given by mediums is that your deceased loved one can communicate with you in more nonverbal ways: through the form of butterflies flying around you, coins dropping out of your purse or pockets, birds flying near your home, or lights turning on and off. These are supposedly messages of comfort to let you know that your deceased loved one cares for you and is watching over you. How the dead person accomplishes this, or why the messages come in these forms, usually is not explained.

ANGELS: THE GOOD AND THE BAD

Angels are popular in New Age beliefs and among those who practice the occult. Angel cards were very big in the New Age in the 1980s. These cards featured images of angels and daily meditative thoughts.

In most non-Christian views today, all angels are seen as good. There is little or no recognition of bad or fallen angels. Many believe that everyone has a guardian angel and that it is okay to contact this guardian angel. Workshops and books abound on contacting angels, working with your guardian angel, and discovering the "inner" angel.

Scripture tells us of two kinds of angels: good angels who serve God and fallen angels who rebelled and went with Satan. Fallen angels are considered to be demons or evil spirits. There is some disagreement on this, but for the purposes of this discussion, demons, evil spirits, and fallen angels will be considered to be the same beings.

Psalm 104:4 and Hebrews 1:14 teach that angels are spirits. Since contacting spirits is forbidden, this would include contacting angels. Good angels are under God's authority and serve at his command, not ours. If angel contact is attempted, a fallen angel will no doubt be happy to oblige, disguised as a "good" angel. (Remember 2 Corinthians 11:14, which states that Satan disguises himself as an angel of light.) It is reasonable to conclude that demons can do this as well.

GHOSTS AND THE DEAD

One of the top questions I get from teens is about haunted houses or seeing ghosts. The Bible is clear that dead people cannot hang around after death. Jesus' story in Luke 16 about the rich man and the beggar who both go to specific places immediately after death illustrates this. The rich man goes to a place of torment and the beggar Lazarus goes to Abraham's bosom. Paul says that to die would mean to be with Christ. In Philippians 1:21, he says that "to live is Christ and to die is gain." In verse 23, Paul makes the statement that he desires "to depart and be with Christ." In 2 Corinthians 5:8, Paul says that he would "prefer to be away from the body and at home with the Lord" (NIV).

To believe in ghosts means accepting that people could still hang around in some form after death. How is this possible based on what the Bible teaches? No biblical accounts verify actual ghosts. In Luke 24:37, the two men from Emmaus thought they were seeing a ghost when the resurrected Jesus suddenly appeared to them, and in Matthew 14:26, Jesus' disciples thought they were seeing a ghost when they saw Jesus walking on water. But these incidents reflect man's belief in ghosts, not the Bible's. If a ghost could exist, it would mean that the dead person had some kind of power over death and was able to avoid going anywhere else after dying. This does not make sense in light of the biblical accounts and statements.

Many television shows air dramatic accounts of haunted houses, showing strange lights in windows or moving doors, or offer photographs of people with surreal lights around them. What does this mean? If someone hears the story of a ghost, or sees one of those television shows or photographs of a haunted house, four explanations are possible:

1. The account was imagined.

2. The account, TV show, or photograph is a hoax.

3. There is a natural explanation for what occurred or

is seen (perhaps with the film processing in photographs, for example).

4. The source is demonic.

Keeping these four explanations in mind will help to
give you confidence in responding if your kids bring up
these alleged ghosts and hauntings.

THE MEDIUMS

I started getting questions from teens about medium John
Edward soon after his show debuted on the Sci-Fi channel.
Edward is young and rather hip, laughs at himself, and is
personable and appealing. He discovered through guided
visualization that he had five spirit guides plus a master
guide.[13] After receiving information from his recently
deceased mother, Edward was convinced of after-death
communication and eventually went to work as a medium
full-time. According to Edward, he gets sounds, images,
and sensations from the spirits since they cannot speak, and
who he says vibrate at very high rates, making communication difficult.[14]

Though Edward claims to be Catholic, he realizes that
the Catholic Church opposes what he does.[15] He claims
that his relationship with God is important and that his
"connection" to God has never wavered.[16] Edward has
priests and nuns as clients, and says in his book that he
prays the rosary and does a meditation before doing spirit
contact.[17]

Another popular medium, Sylvia Browne, often refers
to God and even to Christ during her many stints on talk
shows. Because of this, many believe her to be a Christian.

This is yet another reminder to be aware that simply referring to "God" and "Jesus" doesn't mean a person is a Christ-follower.

Browne claims she was born psychic and that her psychic grandmother helped her understand her gifts. At the tender age of eight, Browne met her spirit guide, whom she calls Francine, and who told Sylvia, "I come from God, Sylvia." Browne relies on her spirit guide, Francine, for most of her information about the "other side," and Francine is the main source of information for Browne's *Journey of the Soul Series*.

Browne gives her background as Catholic, Jewish, Episcopalian, and Lutheran, but she rejects any religion with "harsh" and "cruel" concepts such as "sin, guilt, and retribution."[18] In 1986, Browne founded her own church, *Novus Spiritus*, which is based on her "Christian Gnostic theology with shades of many other religions blended in."[19] According to Browne, "Gnostic" means one "is a seeker of truth and knowledge about God," and is not a seeker of "dogma."[20] She also preaches that, in order to be elevated to any spiritual level, one must have "total knowledge."[21]

Browne's *Journey of the Soul Series* presents complex teachings on God, creation, good and evil, death, spirits, angels, reincarnation, and other theological topics. Although Browne denies the pantheistic belief that all is God,[22] she does say that we are a "divine spark" that emanated from God, and that everyone has his or her own "God center."[23] Moreover, she states that God does not punish or judge, and there is no hell.[24] It does not matter in Browne's theology if Jesus is the Son of God, because *everyone* is.[25] According to Browne, Jesus did not die on the cross, but came to bring wisdom.[26]

A believer in reincarnation, Browne states that this life is her fifty-fourth and last one.[27] Each planet has its own Other Side; Earth's Other Side is superimposed on our reality, with a higher vibrational frequency. People on Earth are actually ghosts in the world of spirits, but are less alive than the spirits, who are really the ones who are fully alive.[28] (This idea is also found in the movie *The Others.*) All spirits on the Other Side are thirty years old, but they choose their own physical attributes.[29] Those who come to Earth do so to learn, watched over by spirits from the Other Side.[30]

Another famous medium is James Van Praagh (also a coproducer of the television show *Ghost Whisperer,* about a young woman who communicates with the dead), who realized as a first-grader that he was psychic when he knew that a car had hit his teacher's son before the teacher heard about it. This Catholic schoolteacher told young James that he had been given a gift and that he was "one of God's messengers."[31] He also saw auras around people as a young child.[32] Raised staunchly Catholic, Van Praagh nevertheless found himself wondering whether God really existed, and if the Bible was true.[33] After asking God to prove his existence, Van Praagh, at age eight, saw a large, glowing hand, pulsating with light, coming down toward him as he lay in bed, and he knew this was God.[34] Van Praagh continued to have paranormal experiences, including contact with a spirit via the Ouija board, as he sought answers about the afterlife.

To please his mother, Van Praagh enrolled in a seminary as preparation for the priesthood, but he had many doubts about the teachings. During a meditation at the seminary, Van Praagh realized that God is love and is nonjudgmental, and that he is within us. After this, Van Praagh left the seminary and the Catholic Church.[35]

A few years later, after a stretch in broadcasting, Van Praagh received a reading from a medium who told him that he had mediumistic abilities and that the spirits would use him.[36] After reading books on how to develop psychic and mediumistic abilities, he practiced these techniques for about a year, increasing his psychic sensitivity.[37] Like Edward, Van Praagh states that doing spirit contact gave him a strong sense of love and joy, and requests for his services led him to do this full-time.[38]

Van Praagh believes that all creatures, both human and nonhuman, are made of the "same God spark."[39] God is mankind's very "essence," and though many have come representing the "light of God," everyone is divine.[40] Van Praagh believes in reincarnation, discussing this at length in his books. The soul's journey after death, he claims, involves an intermediate astral world, then progresses to a higher level where it is more "enlightened," and finally reaches the "true heaven world."[41]

In order to communicate with the dead, Van Praagh says he must raise his vibrational level, and he must concentrate, since he does not hear the spirits at a normal conversational level.[42] He opens his mind to the thoughts of the spirits and repeats exactly what he perceives.[43] Like both Edward and Browne, Van Praagh believes everyone has spirit guides. Preparation for readings involves the meditation (centering) most psychics practice, and Van Praagh gives instructions on various meditations in his books.

THE "DEAD" HAVE A HARD TIME COMMUNICATING

It is interesting to note that Edward, Browne, and Van Praagh all freely admit that they are not always accurate.[44] Indeed, Browne writes that no psychic has 100 percent accuracy, and that 70 percent is above average.[45]

Edward claims that what the spirits give him is often in symbolic language and therefore difficult to interpret. His explanation for this difficulty is the higher vibrations of the spirits.[46] There is no way to authenticate this information; there is only the word of the mediums and others who teach this concept. Edward talks about the spirits playing "psychic charades,"[47] and Browne similarly states that the spirits don't speak, but instead communicate by pantomime in a sort of "divine game of charades."[48] Thus, the mediums can always explain away inaccurate information as being due to difficulties in communication from the spirit world, or misinterpretation of the symbolic language.

This raises questions: Why do recently dead people have trouble communicating? Where do they get these objects that they show Edward and Van Praagh? And why would these spirits have any special wisdom just because they are dead?

THE SUPERIORITY OF GOD'S ANGELS AND PROPHETS

In contrast to the difficulties of the mediums in understanding the dead are the clear and accurate messages given by the prophets and angels of God in the Bible. When God spoke through his prophets, or sent messages via his angels, the words and messages were clear; there was no need to interpret gestures, images, or pantomime. Angels, who are spirits, were able to speak distinctly.

It is reasonable to conclude that information from God or approved by God will not be confusing nor will it be difficult to transmit or understand.

This discussion on spiritism continues in the next chapter.

BRINGING IT HOME

Use these ideas to help your child understand the nature of angels as spirits versus the nature of man as a human creature.

- Read Hebrews 1:14 together, which declares that angels are "ministering spirits." Ask your child to tell you what he thinks an angel is like.

- Hebrews 2:7 distinguishes humans from the angels when stating that God has made humans "for a little while lower than the angels," and verse 16 teaches that Jesus did not come for the angels. So here is a clear distinction between man and angels. Talk with your child about this distinction.

- Make sure your child understands that many people (especially mediums) refer to dead people as "spirits" and the place where they go as "the world of spirits." This is not accurate in light of the Bible since only angels are spirits.

- Explore biblical accounts of angels with your child to show how they speak for God (good angels) or align with Satan (fallen angels). Here are a few passages to begin with: The angel Gabriel is sent to Mary to tell her she would bear Jesus the Savior (see Luke 1:26–28); an angel appears to Joseph to tell him that Mary would have Jesus (see Matthew 1:20–21); angels are sent to announce the birth of Jesus to the shepherds (see Luke 2:9–13); an angel warns Joseph to flee to Egypt to avoid Herod's attempt to kill Jesus (see Matthew 2:13). Point out that in none of these instances (or in any other cases from the Bible) do any of these people attempt to contact an angel. God is always the one who decides when to send angels.

13

Angels of Light: Deception from Beyond

Part Two

I do spirit contact over years and enjoy and association with them, for a lot of cases i found the evidence what they told me and historic truth. it is the time to open your mind to accept the truth for the aspect of achieving wisdom.[1]

When I had lucid dreams I often contacted a spirit guide, it was always the same person. tall, white long hair, looked pretty strong, and had green eyes. he used to tell me I could share all my problems with him, and he would guide me. he would often appear to me, and until recently after almost a year of not lucid dreaming, he appeared again and said, 'hey, its been a long time.' he looks pretty friendly. who is he? he's got this "wizard" type of look.[2]

*W*hat do you say if your child sees a documentary on a haunting, or hears a story about a visit from a dead person? What if the information given by a medium is accurate? These questions have answers.

WHAT IF THE INFORMATION IS CORRECT?

Sometimes mediums pass on accurate information. This makes it seem like they are hearing from the dead. Skeptics who have assessed mediums and replicated what they do have concluded that they are performing trickery or fishing for information.[3] Some say that Edward and other mediums are practicing a technique known as a "cold reading" in which initials or numbers are tossed out to the audience that someone eventually will respond to. Skeptics also point out that people notice the hits more than the misses, although they say the misses outweigh the hits. Believers in mediums are convinced by the hits, and this often seems to be enough for them. While agreeing that these methods might be used by some mediums, I think convincing people that mediums are frauds is a waste of time.

The issue is often framed in terms of "either-or." Either the mediums are frauds or they are receiving information from the dead. But must it be one or the other? Could it be neither—or a combination? How does one explain that the mediums' accurate information is not from God?

Deuteronomy 13:1-3 advises that if a "sign or wonder" comes to pass from a prophet or a "dreamer of dreams," but then that prophet or dreamer asks that you follow other gods, not to listen to what this prophet or dreamer says. If the medium gives correct information but has spiritual beliefs contradictory to God's Word, then what he or she is saying cannot be from God. Both Browne and Van Praagh deny the biblical God. Browne denies Jesus' death on the cross and denies a need for judgment on sin. Browne, Van Praagh, and Edward all believe in reincarnation, a doctrine that contradicts salvation by grace alone since reincarnation teaches that one can improve spiritually and morally through living several lives, thus nullifying the need for salvation.

Can the ability to hear from the dead be a gift from God? James 1:17 states that only "good and perfect" gifts come from God. God would not give someone a gift for a special skill that he himself condemns. Even if the information is correct, it cannot be from God, as the mediums are engaged in a practice forbidden by God, and they espouse beliefs that go against God's Word.

What Edward, Browne, and Van Praagh describe about their experiences is similar to what I studied and experienced as an astrologer and as a student of psychic techniques. When reading astrological charts, I did on occasion receive startlingly accurate information that seemed as though it was being fed into my mind. I usually went into an altered state of consciousness[4] and felt a beam of energy connect me to the chart (not the client). I also did many charts for clients who were not physically present, ruling out the possibility of reading body language or being led by the client. If I was able to come up with some specific accurate information this way without practicing the techniques described by the skeptics, is it not possible the same thing is happening to the psychics and mediums?

Due to the spiritual beliefs they hold, their meditative practices, and their training as psychics, mediums may be opening themselves up to information from … somewhere. If it is not the dead, then who is giving information when it is specific and correct? The 2 Corinthians 11:14 passage about Satan disguising himself as an angel of light certainly makes it seem possible that demons can disguise themselves as the dead and relay information.

SAUL AND SAMUEL AND THE MEDIUM AT ENDOR

Many Christians are puzzled by the meaning of the story of King Saul and the medium (or witch) at Endor in 1 Samuel 28:3–23. Saul had banned mediums, but desperate for advice due to the advancing Philistine army and God's silence on what to do, he seeks out a medium to call up Samuel's spirit. Samuel appears and tells Saul that he disobeyed God in not destroying the Amalekites in a previous battle, that Israel will fall to the Philistines, and that Saul and his sons will die in battle the next day. This passage cannot be taken to endorse spirit contact at all, especially when 1 Chronicles 10:13 states clearly: "So Saul died for his unfaithfulness which he had committed against the LORD, because he did not keep the word of the LORD, and also because he consulted a medium for guidance" (NKJV).

There is debate as to whether Samuel was really called up by the medium or whether this was a demonic spirit. However, the Bible specifically states that Samuel appeared. Furthermore, Samuel's accurate and specific predictions about the deaths of Saul and his sons, and about Israel's defeat by the Philistines, indicate that this was not a demonic spirit, since only God knows the end from the beginning (see Isaiah 46:10) and according to Deuteronomy 18:22, only prophets from God give prophecies or predictions that are consistently 100 percent correct. We can conclude that God brought up Samuel for the specific purpose of rebuking Saul and condemning his actions.

God had some pretty harsh words for false prophets who were telling their dreams as though they came from God. This is not too different from claiming to receive messages from the dead and saying that God approves of this, when God has clearly forbidden such contact. This is what God had to say about the prophets who presented their dreams as coming from God, when they weren't:

> I have heard what the prophets say who prophesy lies in my name. They say, "I had a dream! I had a dream!" How long will this continue in the hearts of these lying prophets, who prophesy the delusions of their own minds? They think the dreams they tell one another will make my people forget my name, just as their fathers forgot my name through Baal worship. Let the prophet who has a dream tell his dream, but let the one who has my word speak it faithfully. For what has straw to do with grain?" declares the LORD. "Is not my word like fire," declares the LORD, "and like a hammer that breaks a rock in pieces?" (Jeremiah 23:25–29 NIV)

Information from God does not come through spirit contact. And the only person who truly came back from the dead was Jesus Christ. As he said, "I am the first and the last, and the living One; and I was dead, and behold, I am alive forevermore, and I have the keys of death and of Hades" (Revelation 1:17–18).

TESTING THE SPIRITS

The Bible instructs believers to "test" the spirits. Messages from the "dead," from the spirits, and from channeled entities never encourage people to believe the Bible, never urge people to trust Christ for salvation, and often openly contradict God's Word or even speak derisively of Christ as Savior.

Contacting spirits is spiritism and is forbidden by God in Leviticus 19:31; 20:6; 20:27; Deuteronomy 18:11; 2 Kings 21:6; 23:24; 2 Chronicles 33:6; and Isaiah 8:19, among other places. The Isaiah passage puts it clearly: "When men tell you to consult mediums and spiritists, who whisper and mutter, should not a people inquire of their God? Why consult the dead on behalf of the living?" (NIV).

The story of the rich man and Lazarus in Luke 16:19–31 implies that the dead cannot contact the living. Consulting the dead, a practice called necromancy, was done usually for purposes of divination and seeking out the advice of pagan gods. Perhaps for that reason, God considers consulting mediums and spiritists as spiritual adultery in Leviticus 20:6.

The next chapter will examine one specific tool for spirit contact, the well-known and infamous Ouija board.

BRINGING IT HOME

One of the best ways to handle this topic with kids is to look at Jesus' explicit account of the rich man and the beggar, Lazarus, in Luke 16:19–31.

- Read this account with your child. Some believe that this is a parable; others disagree, because it is not presented as a parable and because Jesus gives the name of one of the characters, which he does not do in any of his parables. Whether it is a parable or not, the truth of what Jesus states remains the same.

- Ask your child to tell the story in his own words.

- Ask: Is the rich man allowed to go back or able to cross over to where Lazarus is (or vice versa)? Is there any indication here that a dead person can communicate with the living in any way?

- Look at Revelation 1:18. Jesus has power over death. There is no indication in the Bible that dead people are given power to "come back" or to communicate with the living. Ask your child: If God so strongly forbids contact with spirits and with the dead, does it makes sense that he would allow dead people to communicate with us?

14

THE OUIJA BOARD:
DIALING FOR DANGER?

First of all, even though I am psychic, there are a few
things I *don't* or *won't* do when I receive information.
First, you won't get me anywhere near a few of the
psychic tools (such as a Ouija board) that people use. As
a psychic, one of the first things you learn is
discernment. Such tools, like a Ouija board or meditative
trances, basically act like an open door for any spirit out
there to walk through.[1]

My 15 year old daughter, it has recently been revealed to
me, has spent time using the Ouija board at a friend's
house, and her friend's mother did a Reiki massage on her
and has been telling her she has these "good" spirits
around her protecting her.[2]

i just wanted to ask some questions to the ouija board .How could i do that. Im having hard trouble now and i need some of my questions answer. Could you please help me.[3]

At a New Age fair I once attended, a workshop was given by a medium on how to contact the dead. She spent several minutes at the beginning warning people against using the Ouija board, because she said that such a tool was like using a telephone without knowing whom you were calling.

Most people are familiar with the Ouija board manufactured by Parker Brothers. This board is eighteen inches by about twelve inches with a series of numbers printed at the top, and the alphabet arranged in a semicircle of two lines. The words *Yes* and *No* are off to each side, with "Good Bye" printed at the bottom. A triangular pointing device, called a *planchette,* comes with the board. One is to place the hands very lightly on the planchette, ask questions, and wait for the planchette to spell out answers via the numbers, alphabet, or answering "yes" or "no." In some books, the Ouija board is categorized under automatic writing.

There is a story that the name "Ouija" derives from the French word *oui* for "yes," combined with the German word *ja* for "yes." This would mean that "Ouija" translates as "yes, yes," perhaps an invitation to spirit contact.

I never used a Ouija board until after college, but in college some girls in my dorm got very scared using it. It is hard to know what really happened, but they were so frightened that one of them came to get my roommate, who was the freshman advisor for the dorm. I followed her down the hall into the room where several of the girls were crying from fear. They said they had asked the board who it was, and the answer came back, "I am Alpha and Omega." Then they claimed the lights came on and went off again.

One time after college, I was using the board with a housemate. At first, the messages were friendly, but they soon became increasingly hostile. The planchette was moving so fast that another housemate had to take down the letters. Finally, the friend who was doing the board with me stood up, declaring that there was something evil in the room and she was going upstairs.

Jane Roberts, author of the channeled *Seth* series, explained that Seth began his contact while she and her husband were experimenting with a Ouija board in 1963. This led to Roberts feeling compelled to speak Seth's words aloud, which eventually resulted in her becoming a direct channel for Seth by letting him speak through her.[4]

Few objects have so many alarming tales about them as the Ouija board. I am often told by teens that you cannot burn a Ouija board, or if you do, it "comes back." This tale of the board coming back has become a sort of urban legend, giving the board itself an almost mythic status and more menacing power than it possesses, qualities which attract some people. However, it is not the board itself that is the problem; rather, it is using the board to contact spirits that is the issue.

ISN'T THE OUIJA BOARD JUST A GAME?

Because it is made by Parker Brothers and sold in toy stores, many believe the Ouija board is just a game, like Monopoly or Clue. But the origins of the Ouija board go far back in history and have nothing to do with games.

The Ouija board operates on the same principle as a pendulum and as automatic writing: One asks questions when holding an object and then waits for the object to move a certain way, or, in the case of automatic writing, to write out answers. This kind of divination goes back to ancient cultures (note the previous reference in Hosea 4:12).

The use of such pre-Ouija board devices may go as far back as 500 BC to China and Greece, and to third-century Rome.[5] In the 1800s, a popular practice for divination was *table tipping* or *table rapping*. This involved people around a table, lightly touching it, asking questions, and waiting for the table to tap or rap the prearranged number of times for "yes" or "no" or to spell out answers using an alphabet numerical equivalence system. To simplify this rather ungainly method, in 1853, a French spiritualist, M. Planchette, invented the triangular object that came to be called a *planchette*. This device operated as a miniature table on three legs, one of which was a pencil that would write out answers as the planchette moved.[6] In effect, he created a smaller version of the larger tables used for table rapping, and provided a way for messages to be spelled out.

The modern Ouija board got its start in the United States with inventor Elijah Bond, who first filed for a patent in 1890 for a "Ouija or Egyptian luck-board."[7] Baltimore resident William Fuld bought the rights in 1892 and was granted a patent for an improved pointer[8] (Fuld's name appears today at the top of the board). The board was known as the Oriole Talking Board until, according to Fuld, the board itself advised him that it should be named the "Ouija Board,"[9] the name used by Bond when he had first filed for a patent. Upon the board's further advice, Fuld built a factory and began manufacturing the board quite successfully, all the while denying that he was a spiritualist and insisting that he had not consulted the board since he had taken its advice to build a business around it.[10] (Ironically, Fuld died in 1927 as a result of a fall from the roof of the very building the board had advised him to construct.)[11]

The popularity of the board peaked in 1920 when grieving relatives of soldiers killed in World War I used the board in attempts to contact their deceased loved ones.

After the war, the board had times of up and down sales, peaking again during World War II and later in the 1960s. In 1966, the games manufacturer, Parker Brothers, bought the rights to the Ouija board, and in 1976, sales of the board topped the sales of their best-selling board game, Monopoly.[12]

In recent years, Parker Brothers has run television ads for the board at Christmas with the cryptic statement, "It's just a game—or is it?"

What Is Really Happening with the Board?

Most people ask questions of the board, believing that they will get answers from the "spirit of the board," a deceased relative or friend, their guardian angel, or some other disembodied guide.

Theories abound about what happens when people consult the Ouija board. Some believe that it is merely a matter of the players moving the planchette on purpose to give answers. Others believe that the spelled-out messages are from the players' unconscious minds. A third group believes that they are actually receiving messages from dead people or from some type of discarnate spirit.

However, if one believes that spirit contact can elicit the responses of fallen angels, a fourth view should be the biblical one—that in some cases, the responses are from fallen angels. This would explain some of the strange and dangerous experiences people have had when using the board.

Even many of those who believe the board merely passes on messages from the unconscious believe it to be dangerous because they think that participants can become obsessed with the board, or that players may be unable to handle the messages they receive. Most psychics and mediums advise against using the board, believing that you are opening yourself up to negative spirits who seek to use or control you. This is true, although the "negative spirits" are actually fallen angels.

The objection of psychics to the Ouija board is that when it is used by the inexperienced and ignorant, it is not a safe method for spirit contact. Of course, according to the Bible, there is no such thing as an acceptable or safe way to contact spirits.

THE BOARD'S DECEPTIONS

Despite the warnings of many, advocates for the Ouija board make it seem that one can use the board carefully. The guise taken by Satan and fallen angels is not necessarily one of menace or danger, but is often moralistic. Indeed, it is common to find psychics or those who contact or channel spirits praying before their sessions. They may even say the Lord's Prayer and announce that they are Christians. In many cases, they may believe they are. Claims to Christianity notwithstanding, God's Word is the standard, not what a practitioner says or does.

A bold recommendation to pray before using the board actually came from a spirit calling himself Thomas who was contacted by a woman using the board in Canada in the 1970s. She eventually continued communications with Thomas via automatic writing. Thomas, according to this woman, recommends praying before using the Ouija board.[13] Thomas even offered up a sample prayer, addressing God as "Keeper of the Universe" and asking for protection from "negative forces."[14] This is typical of the moralistic and sanctimonious advice you will find in channeled messages from various spirits. Most of them are superior and patronizing toward humans, and they attempt to sound moral and spiritual, thus reflecting the arrogance and deception of their master, Satan.

The spirit called Thomas gives himself away, however, in stating that in the future "people are going to have a different kind of religion" and that the "Dark Age of religion is slowly losing its grip and the church leaders are no longer able to keep so many people's minds fettered."[15] Here you see Satan's hatred for the church. Thomas, waxing warmly to his task as spiritual consultant, continues by saying that in between his returns to Earth he goes "to a higher level" that is "less cluttered with the problems of physical life" where he can bask in "purity of thought."[16] This would be laughable if not for the knowledge of how many are misled by such messages from the spirit world. Thomas advises that the best way to prepare for death, which is really a "glorious beginning," is to study and accept reincarnation.[17] Such statements about death are common in readings from psychics, in teachings from supposed aliens and advanced spiritual masters, and in channeled messages from spirits.

In an online interview, well-known Pagan Selena Fox explained how she came to become the priestess of a an occult magical group. During a meditation, she received a message instructing her to walk along a street where she would see a sign. She did this and came across a sign advertising a psychic fair for the following day. She continues, "Unbeknownst to me then, a group had been working with a Ouija board doing spirit communication and had a message come through that said the group would deepen when the priestess would show up and that their priestess was coming." She attended the fair and met the people who had received this message from the board, soon becoming the priestess of the group.[18]

CAN THE BOARD PREDICT?

Stories after stories claim predictions made via the Ouija board. It is important to keep several things in mind when hearing such tales.

First, the prediction may have been very general and then applied specifically. For example, a prediction that someone will get a surprise at work could be followed by something that was indeed surprising, suggesting that the prediction was accurate. However, it only appears to be a prediction fulfilled because the prediction was so general. A surprise at work could be anything from a dropped coffee cup to an unexpected bonus. Someone looking for a surprise is likely to find something that fills the bill.

Second, a prediction might be made about something that would have happened anyway. Predictions may be about meeting someone, traveling, changing jobs, getting money, or other things that are all part of life and many experience these things. When one evaluates the messages from the board, usually no specifics are given for these future events, or if they are, they are wrong.

Third, it could simply be a matter of coincidence.

Last, but certainly not the least, is the possibility of a demonic hand in the event predicted. Some Christians would disagree with me here, but I believe it is possible that in a small number of cases, demonic influence on people may cause the predicted event to come about.

Satan does not know the future, except what the Bible says about his future defeat. Therefore, predictions of the future with an occult source, whether from psychics, mediums, astrologers, the Ouija board, pendulums, or other forms of divination, will usually be very general, faulty if specific, applicable to many people, or a coincidence.

A good example of this comes from the statement of the woman who used the board to communicate with the spirit calling itself Thomas. The woman stated that Thomas often tried to forewarn her of good or bad events, but that it wasn't "until after the event we were able to interpret his remarks."[19] In other words, the prediction did not do any good because it could be understood only in light of the event after it occurred.

Evaluation of the history and purpose of the Ouija board clearly marks it as an object to be avoided.

Contacting spirits and attempts to contact the dead make up a large part of paranormal activities and are one of the three categories of occult practices. Other areas not specifically mentioned in the Bible are crucial to occult beliefs and practices. These areas are examined in the next chapter.

BRINGING IT HOME

Even if your child has never seen a Ouija board, the chances are high that he or she will encounter it one day. Many kids use Ouija boards at sleepovers or parties and never tell their parents about it. Use these ideas to warn your child about the Ouija board.

- Tell your child that the Ouija board was not invented by Parker Brothers and was never a toy or game, but designed specifically for contacting the dead. Ask him to tell you how that fact makes him feel about the board.

- Ask your child if the board itself can answer questions—and if not, ask whom she thinks is actually providing the answers.

- Ask: If the board gives answers, then what is causing this? Go over the possibilities mentioned in this chapter.

- Keep in mind that this subject matter might be scary to children and even to some sensitive teens. Reassure them that Jesus is more powerful than any evil angels and that we do not need to be afraid of these things.

15

Auras, the Astral Plane, Astral Travel, Energy, and Symbols

*[W]e use the term Universal Energy/Universal
Life Force because Reiki healers are all different
religions and do not have the same belief system.*[1]

*I don't play about with energy for the power,
the only times I can remember when I actually
put the energy to a purpose is for shielding.*[2]

$\mathcal{T}$he invisible powers of the paranormal are becoming
more accepted and popular every day. People readily believe
statements about energies, even though there is no way to
verify their nature or existence. The teachings on these
invisible energies do not fit neatly into any category, yet
they are key to occult and New Age beliefs and practices.

AURAS

Many psychics or those who claim psychic abilities maintain that they see auras. An aura is a field of "subtle energy" surrounding a person. Some teachings about auras claim the auras come in different colors, with each color indicating something about the person's emotional, physical, and spiritual state.

In my first psychic-development class, one class member would stand against a white wall while the other class members practiced seeing the aura. We were told to let our eyes blur a bit and not look directly at anything. Some said they saw something; others saw nothing. Naturally, an unfocused gaze could cause your eyes to play tricks on you.

Some people claim that the halos around Jesus, his disciples, and various saints and angels in old paintings represent their auras. It is believed that painting halos was first done in ancient Greece and Rome, then borrowed by Christians in the early years of the church and during the Middle Ages for angels and the saints. Greek artists brought the halo technique into India during the reign of Alexander the Great, and Buddhist artists adopted it in their depictions of Buddha and Buddhist saints.[3] Halos in paintings are pictorial representations of the spiritual power or status of a figure; there is no evidence that it signifies a belief in auras.

THE ASTRAL PLANE, ASTRAL BODY, AND ASTRAL TRAVEL

Belief in several levels or planes of reality or existence is quite common in the occult. Some groups have named these levels, from the highest down: causal, spiritual, mental, astral, and material. What exists on the causal plane works its way down through the other planes, finally becoming reality in the material level. At death, the soul passes through the planes in reverse. The lowest plane is always the physical or material realm. As the planes progress from the physical to the causal, the planes become more "spiritual." This Gnostic example of dualism between matter and spirit is common in occult thinking.

The second level from the material, the astral plane, is referred to in virtually all occult ideologies. The astral is usually considered to be the plane of existence immediately beyond the physical. Magicians claim to work on the astral plane, and those who contact the dead often believe that "ghosts" are on the astral plane. Some believe the Akashic Records, the "records of what everyone has done and said," are part of the astral plane. Many psychics believe they are accessing the Akashic Records when they do a reading. The astral is not always considered good or safe, and may contain negativity and troubled spirits.

The *astral self* is believed to separate from the body at death. However, many occult teachings hold that the astral self can leave the body while the person is still alive. Those who allege out-of-body experiences (OBEs) may believe they are practicing astral projection—a technique whereby the astral self separates from the body and travels to other physical locations or to the astral realm. In many New Age and occult belief systems, such as Eckankar, astral travel is considered desirable, although potentially dangerous. Astral travel is referred to in ancient practices from Egypt and Tibet, and was also written about by ancient writers such as Plato, Plotinus, and others.[4]

Some claim that in 2 Corinthians 12:1–5, Paul is speaking of an out-of-body or astral experience. However, in that passage, Paul says that he does not know if he was in his body or not, so the value of this as an astral or out-of-body experience is diminished from the start. Second, this is a revelation and experience that God initiated and gave to Paul; Paul did not seek this out or initiate it. Third, Paul did not reveal what he saw because he was not permitted (see v. 4). Fourth, this experience or visionary revelation is not the point of the passage, but is used to make another point, that Paul cannot boast of anything because he is weak, and God keeps Paul humble through his weakness (see vv. 6–10). This passage does not endorse astral travel; using it as such is a gross misuse and twisting of the passage.

Astral projection is also used by those who call themselves *psychic vampires.* Psychic vampires believe they can leave their body and, in astral form, secretly feed off the spirit or energy of other people.

There is no clear evidence that astral projection is real, although stories from those who claim to practice it make it *seem* real (including this writer, who experienced astral projection frequently). However, there is the possibility that it is a spiritual deception or hallucination. Whatever the case, attempting to learn or practice astral projection or travel is not biblical and is an occult practice to avoid assiduously.

ENERGY

If you have ever cared for a toddler, no doubt you sorely wished at some point, while chasing him or her around, that you could have that much energy! Everyone has a certain amount of physical energy depending on age and general health. This kind of energy, which is physical, differs from occult concepts of energy. Going back to ancient times and even in present-day paranormal practices, we find that one of the cornerstones of occult belief is the use of and access to a nonphysical energy or force. In order to understand this, we need to make distinctions between natural or physical energy and nonphysical forms of energy.

A natural force is exerted physically through a material object or by a physical being such as an animal or human. Electrical energy or power is also considered a physical force.

Paranormal force or energy is mystical and unknown, but while it is allegedly infused into everything that exists, it has no physical, quantifiable properties. This force or energy is referred to by various names, such as *universal life force, life force, universal energy, vital energy, healing energy, sacred energy, divine energy, ether, vitalism,* and others.

Terms from other cultures and languages used to describe this energy include *mana, chi, ki,* and *prana.* This belief in a force or energy is often connected to *pantheism,* the belief that God is all and all is God (or God is energy and all is the energy of God), or *monism,* the belief that all is one—everyone is connected by being part of the same force or energy (which may or may not be called God). Pantheism and monism, taken to their logical conclusions, deny any real distinctions between people, nature, or objects. Any god in pantheism must be a force or energy that permeates all creation and cannot be distinguished from it.

Occult practitioners seek this energy through an object, through ritual, by summoning or channeling, or by invoking a spirit. Many believe this energy or force is a natural phenomenon because it is alleged to be a part of nature. For example, some crystals are believed to have healing properties because they supposedly contain healing energy from the earth. However, the paranormal properties of this energy and the esoteric means of harnessing it reveal it to be anything but natural.

These views of energy permeate the occult and popular books and movies. The Force is a prime example. In the

movie *Star Wars: The Empire Strikes Back,* Yoda, speaking
of the Force, says, "Its energy surrounds us and binds us.
Luminous beings are we, not this crude matter. You must
feel the Force around you. Here, between you, me ... the
tree ... the rock. Yes, even between the land and the
ship."[5]

Not only is this teaching a mystical pantheistic energy,
but the statement that we are "luminous beings" and not
"crude matter" is very gnostic. As New Agers like to say,
"we are spirits [confined] in a body." But this is not biblical. Man is a spirit/soul *and* a body. The fact that Jesus
incarnated in flesh and bodily rose from the grave was a slap
in the face to the body/spirit duality taught by the Gnostics.
John refutes this Gnostic teaching in 1 John 4:2 when he
says, "*every spirit that confesses that Jesus Christ has come in
the flesh is from God,*" because the Gnostics were saying
Jesus did not come in a body.

In contrast to these magical and mythical views, the
Bible speaks of life, not a life force or universal energy.
This life is experiential for man and is an inherent part of
him as a living being, with God as the source—rather than
life being a vitality or magical force separate from man.[6] In
the ancient Near East, men tried to link with "forces of
life" through nature deities or magical incantations and
rituals; in the Bible, on the other hand, life is discovered
through a right relationship with God, and through God's
Word and wisdom.[7]

God and Energy

God is a personal being and is not a force, nor a part of
creation. Although he is Creator, he is distinct from his

creation. Therefore, humanity cannot access God as an energy power source as though he is just another element of nature, or as if he is a supernatural force we invoke at will.

Likewise, the power of the Holy Spirit in a believer's life is not a force to manage at his or her disposal. Such a view goes against the very nature of the Holy Spirit, who is God, the third person of the Trinity, not a force or energy. It would be reasonable to characterize occult powers as a distorted counterfeit of the Holy Spirit.

Many of those who practice occult magic believe that biblical figures such as Moses were magicians. The evidence for this is that Moses carried a staff, performed many miracles, and parted the Red Sea. To occultists, the staff represents a wand or magical rod. They also believe that Moses must have learned powerful Egyptian magic. They do not accept the Bible's teaching that Moses was only able to execute these supernormal feats because God performed them through Moses, or because he gave Moses miraculous ability to perform them.

As for Jesus, many occultists see his miracles as acts of magic. In rejecting the biblical concept of God, those in the occult mistake God's power, which is part of his being, as a magical energy that can be summoned or accessed. God is not made up of parts and is not a divisible being. His power, his love, his justice, his mercy, and his other attributes exist in balance within the nature and character of God. There is no power emanating from God, like a magical force, that humans can summon or channel.

Any practice that advocates the manipulation or access of a paranormal energy or force is occultic and is to be scrupulously avoided, no matter what biblical terms may be used to promote it.

SYMBOLS

Many parents are concerned with symbols and wonder about their meaning and appropriateness. It's important not to overreact to symbols as though the symbols themselves are inherently evil, but some crucial pieces of information about symbols can offer you a balanced and sound view of this subject.

Symbols are fluid in their use and meaning. Their meaning depends on the culture and time in which they exist and on the meaning ascribed to them by the group using the symbol. The backgrounds of many symbols are murky, and often the use of a symbol changes or crosses over from one culture or belief to another. For example, the pentagram or pentacle, which is widely used by Witches/Wiccans today, once represented the five wounds of Christ. The swastika of Nazism comes from many ancient cultures and stood for various things—the motion of the sun through the sky, the four directions, the sun's rays, and so on. No one is sure of its true origins. Animals have been used as symbols in many ways. The phoenix, stag, and unicorn have all been used as symbols in the occult practice of alchemy, and also became Christian symbols. It is virtually impossible to say, for example, that the unicorn or the phoenix always symbolizes the same thing. Symbols must be taken in context of time, culture, and use.

There is disagreement on the occultic nature of some symbols as well as their meaning. For example, the ankh was depicted in Egypt with gods and goddesses and was thought to represent immortal life and the union of male and female. Today it is used by those in the New Age and Witchcraft and in the vampire subculture. Its original meaning may not be known and even now it might have different meanings depending on the beliefs of those who use it.

Religious symbols can be used by any culture and are sometimes misinterpreted by those cultures. The yin-yang black-and-white symbol comes from the Chinese religion of Taoism and signifies the ideal balance of yin and yang forces, but is often misused in Western culture to represent balance or harmony. The original meaning of any symbol may or may not be retained. Therefore, it is wise to be careful with any symbol and not assume anything without first looking at the history, cultural context, and present use of that symbol.

A symbol by itself is merely a symbol. What matters is what it signifies and how it is being interpreted in the present culture. A five-pointed star, a pentacle, is merely a geometric shape and is not inherently evil or dangerous. It is one of many geometric shapes created by God. This shape is also used for stars or snowflakes as Christmas decor or even a sheriff's badge. When it is a snowflake or star or sheriff's badge, however, it is clearly different from the pentacles worn as jewelry by a Wiccan. Therefore, even though a pentacle is merely a geometric figure, Christians should not wear them in such a way to resemble the Wiccan symbol. There is no reason, however, to ban children from drawing five-pointed figures when cutting out snowflakes for Christmas decorations or when crafting a star to top your Christmas tree![8]

JOINING ALL THE THREADS

You now have foundational information to understand the paranormal, how it shows up in Western culture, and what the Bible says about it.

What are some of the best ways to talk to your children about all this? How do you respond to objections? All of this is covered in the next section, beginning with a chapter focusing on the fear of the Lord, for that is the beginning of wisdom. To discuss the occult requires being rooted in a biblical worldview.

Although some suggestions for explaining things to children have been given in the "Bringing It Home" sections at the end of each chapter, the next section will deal with an overall broader approach in communicating with your child, some responses you can make to specific objections your child might have, and equipping and protecting your child.

BRINGING IT HOME

The most essential point to make to your child regarding this chapter would be the personhood and nature of the Trinitarian God. God is not a force or energy, but a personal being, as are Jesus and the Holy Spirit. Go over these points with your child.

- Ask your child if a force like electricity has a mind, intelligence, or will. Can a force have such things? Can a force have love?

- Jesus said that God loved the world so much that he sent Jesus Christ, so that those who believed in him would not perish but live (see John 3:16). Other passages about God's love include Romans 5:8; 8:39; Ephesians 2:4; 1 John 3:1; 4:9–11. Indeed, God *is* the perfect expression of love, because he is love (see 1 John 4:8, 16). Talk with your child about what it means that God is a personal God. Ask: How does knowing God is a personal God affect the way you think about him? About how you receive his love?

- The Holy Spirit is not a force but the third person of the Trinity. He can be lied to (Acts 5:3); he can be grieved (Ephesians 4:30); he has a will (1 Corinthians 12:11); he loves (Romans 15:30); he testifies of Jesus (John 15:26); and he speaks (Acts 8:29; 13:2). Spend some time talking about the difference between the Holy Spirit and the general idea of "spiritual energy." Again, focus on the truth that the Holy Spirit is not only God, but a personal God.

- Discuss these ideas with your child: Although God is present everywhere (omnipresent), because he cannot be contained or limited, he is distinct from creation. He is not part of the world he created nor is he part of his creatures. He is with us, but he is not a part of human nature.

PART THREE:

TALKING TO YOUR KIDS ABOUT THE PARANORMAL

16

TAKING A STAND: THE FEAR OF GOD IS THE BEGINNING OF WISDOM

The fear of the LORD is the beginning of wisdom,
And the knowledge of the Holy One is understanding.
(Proverbs 9:10)

And to man He said, "Behold, the fear
of the Lord, that is wisdom;
And to depart from evil is understanding." (Job 28:28)

The fear of the LORD is clean, enduring forever;
The judgments of the LORD are true; they are
righteous altogether. (Psalm 19:9)

*H*aving a proper attitude is crucial when discussing the areas of the paranormal and occult with your child. Parents should be firm, but definitely not fearful. Equally important is your behavior; be a good role model. It is especially important for parents to know how to go to Scripture and show their children why they are taking the stand they do.

My suggestions are not based on being an expert on raising children, but from my experiences in talking to a lot of teens, preteens, and younger children about these topics.

FOCUS ON GOD'S CHARACTER AND WISDOM

Do not be fearful or intimidated by the paranormal, or you will pass on this fear to your children. No Bible passage teaches us to be afraid of Satan or anything evil. Instead, God tells us to be watchful and cautious, and to fear God, which means to fear the judgment of a righteous God and to hold a deep reverence for his majesty and holiness. In fact, several places in Scripture emphasize, "the fear of the Lord is the beginning of wisdom."[1]

So let's start here, with the fear of the Lord and with his character. This gives a proper perspective of evil because it comes from God's point of view, and reminds us of God's holiness and righteousness. The contrast of God's absolute goodness with the evil of the paranormal should be an encouragement in taking a stand and in responding based on God's goodness, not on what *we* think is good or bad. The standard for goodness is always God's character, which is absolutely good.

If we focus on God's character and the penalty Christ paid for sins, Christians can be calm in their spirits, knowing that God is in charge and that our part is to trust in the Lord and his Word. The watchwords are caution and alertness, not fear and anxiety. We are urged to be prudent (see Proverbs 13:16; 14:8, 15; 18:15; 22:3), sober and alert, and to stand strong in the faith (see 1 Corinthians 16:13; Ephesians 6:18; Colossians 4:2; 1 Thessalonians 5:6): *"Be of sober spirit, be on the alert. Your adversary, the devil, prowls around like a roaring lion, seeking someone to devour"* (1 Peter 5:8). Notice that this passage does not tell the reader to be afraid.

The first four chapters of Proverbs teach about wisdom, and are a good guide for explaining this concept to children. These chapters contrast wisdom from God with the deceptive ways of the world, and admonish us to trust in the Lord and not in our understanding (see Proverbs 3:5–6), and to "watch over [the] heart with all diligence for from it flow the springs of life" (Proverbs 4:23). These chapters are rich with content about the life that is in God's word and wisdom.

Be familiar with the attributes of God's character, passages that urge man to fear him, and Scriptures on God's wisdom, and share these with your children so that they can see his character and righteousness. This will give them an accurate view of God and consequently, a balanced view of the paranormal.

ABSOLUTE GOOD AND EVIL

Understanding God's absolute goodness and righteousness helps us to understand and accept what he forbids as wrong. We can't judge right from wrong without first understanding the standards for right and wrong. Explain to children that we need to see things from God's viewpoint (which we can discover through his Word, the Bible). First John 1:5, which says that God is light and has no darkness at all, is a great place to start. This verse demonstrates that the true God is not part good and part bad like pagan gods, but is wholly good. Because God is wholly and absolutely good, there is a standard by which to measure good and evil. Other passages to read include Numbers 23:19 and Hebrews 6:18, which teach that God does not lie.

Likewise, Scripture teaches that Christ lived a sinless life, and thus was able to be the sacrifice for sins (see Hebrews 4:15; 1 Peter 2:22; 1 John 3:5). Christ was the "true Light" whose life was the "Light of men" and the "darkness did not comprehend it" (John 1:4–5, 9). In Christ, there is both the condemnation of sin and the hope of redemption through faith in him.

Going over the story of Adam and Eve in the garden illustrates how man likes to blur the line between right and wrong (the "Bringing It Home" section at the end of chapter 5 gives some suggestions for this). God declared what was good and told Adam not to eat of the tree of knowledge of good and evil. However, when Eve was tempted, she preferred to believe the lie of the serpent. Adam, even though he had heard God's direct command not to eat from this tree, gave in as well. In essence, Adam and Eve thought they knew better than God in deciding what was good and what was evil. They chose to believe the serpent over God, and rejected what God had said.

This account is good for all ages, especially younger children, because it is so plain and clear-cut in revealing how humans first rebelled against God's goodness. This story also shows the clear consequences of such disobedience and is a model for sinful behavior throughout history.

The following chart displays the occult views of good and evil versus what God says in the Bible:

OCCULT VIEW	GOD'S WORD
No absolute good or evil.	God is absolutely good: "God is light, and in Him there is no darkness at all" (1 John 1:5).
Evil is a force.	Evil is not a force; it is the absence or rejection of good (see John 3:19–20; Matthew 15:18–20).
Evil and good are part of each other.	God and Satan are distinct (see Luke 10:18; Revelation 12:9).
Evil and good will be joined together.	Jesus will cast Satan in the lake of fire (Revelation 20:10).
Balancing good and evil is the goal.	Reject evil (see Ephesians 5:11), and overcome evil with good (see Romans 12:17, 21).
Good and evil are determined subjectively.	God is the standard for good (Matthew 5:48).

SAFE IN CHRIST

It is good for children to be aware of good and evil, and aware of God's condemnation of the paranormal, but it is not appropriate to scare them. Share the passages about being soberminded and watchful and point out that no Bible passage tells us to fear Satan or anyone. First John 4:4 and Romans 8:31 are also helpful in showing that God is *always* more powerful than any of his creations, including Satan. Second Timothy provides another good admonition: "For God has not given us a spirit of fear, but of power, love, and a sound mind" (1:7 NKJV).

The first chapters of Ephesians, Colossians, Hebrews, and Revelation are excellent in declaring the supremacy of Christ (see especially Ephesians 1:18–23; Colossians 1:13–20; Hebrews 1:1–4; Revelation 1:5–8 and 17–18; also, see 1 Peter 3:22). Help your children to memorize a few of the encouraging verses from these passages.

It's important to maintain a delicate balance here. On the one hand, your goal is to warn children without alarming them. On the other, you don't want to downplay or minimize the dangers of the occult. The best way to do this is to be matter of fact, clear and firm without being dramatic, and to constantly point out what God says in his Word.

Be careful not to overstate the perils or evil of the occult. This can actually be appealing to some children and teens who are attracted to danger—who see danger as powerful and the paranormal as something that can provide strength, power, or a way to rebel. Be straightforward with this—tell your children that you understand danger might seem fun or thrilling, but that it does not end up that way. I tell teens that even if they get a thrill at the beginning of dabbling in this area, they are actually being conned by a shrewd deceiver. I also tell them that our actions have consequences. Believers are safe in Christ in the sense that they should not be afraid, but they still suffer the consequences of disobedience to God.

BEING A ROLE MODEL

This might be a good time to throw out that key chain with the rabbit's foot or four-leaf clover! Even if you say that these things are for "fun," children may take it another way. They may think you really do believe in luck or that objects have power to protect them or to attract good things. Children pick up on their parents' behavior and attitudes, and younger children tend to take things literally. They are more apt to imitate behavior than listen to words, especially if they are getting a mixed message.

It might be difficult, but try to eliminate the word *luck* from your vocabulary if you tend to use it. The concept of luck is antithetical to a Christian worldview. Parents, if you read the horoscope column, or take it lightly, please rethink this. I wish I had a nickel for every time a teen said to me, "My mom said I could read the horoscope as long as I didn't believe in it" or "as long as I just read it for fun." Often parents do not realize how these words impact their child or how seriously a child can take them.

Don't set a bad example. Some teens and preteens who read the horoscope column either take it seriously or develop an interest in astrology. Some become dependent on reading it every day. Remember that horoscope columns are written by astrologers or by those who believe in astrology and espouse a worldview totally at odds with a biblical worldview.

TALKING ABOUT SATAN

The topic of Satan is another tricky area, yet you can find a balanced view of Satan in Scripture. Below are some erroneous views of Satan followed by the biblical views. Since some preteens and younger teens seem to think they can get power or strength from Satan, a biblically based view of Satan is important. Use this information at your discretion depending on the child's age and understanding.

False views:

- Satan is misunderstood and was just trying to help Adam and Eve.

- Satan as Lucifer is really the bringer of enlightenment and knowledge (people who hold this view are sometimes called Luciferians).

- Satan is not real or was created by the church to scare people into obeying the church hierarchy (a view held by many Neopagans/Wiccans).

- Satan is merely a symbol for being your own god (view promoted by Anton LaVey, founder of the Church of Satan).

- Satan will defeat God (hardcore satanism).

- Satan is more powerful than God (basis for this view is that God is not destroying evil).

- Satan and God are in an equal power struggle.

Biblical view:

- Satan is a creature (a fallen angel); he is not eternal like God because he has a beginning.

- Satan does not know everything; only God is omniscient.

- Satan tempts man to sin through enticement and deception. See Genesis 3 and the gospel accounts of the temptations of Jesus in the wilderness.

- Point out that Jesus responded to Satan with Scripture each time.

- Satan is a liar. John 8:44 gives us some words from Jesus: "He was a murderer from the beginning, and does not stand in the truth because there is no truth in him. Whenever he speaks a lie, he speaks from his own nature, for he is a liar and the father of lies."

- Satan can disguise himself as good: "No wonder, for even Satan disguises himself as an angel of light" (2 Corinthians 11:14).

- Satan is on a leash and can only do what God allows (see Job 1 where Satan must get God's permission to afflict Job).

- Satan opposes God, but he is not equal to God nor is he God's opposite. God has no opposite because there is only one God.

- Jesus defeated Satan at the cross by atoning for humanity's sins, and he advocates in heaven for believers against the accusations of Satan (Romans 8:34; Hebrews 7:25, 9:24; 1 John 2:1).

- Christ has power and authority over all powers in heaven and on Earth: "And Jesus came up and spoke to them, saying, 'All authority has been given to Me in heaven and on earth'" (Matthew 28:18; see also Ephesians 1:20–21).

Teach your children: "Submit to God. Resist the devil and he will flee" (James 4:7). The key is submitting to God—seeking his will and his way.

Have your children already dabbled in the occult? Some children and teens falsely believe that if they have dabbled in the occult they cannot be forgiven because somehow Satan "owns" them, or they believe God will not forgive them. Some occult groups teach that if one renounces Christ, he or she can never go back to Christ. Show your child what Scripture says about God's total forgiveness through faith in Christ.

TAKING THE HIGH ROAD

Focus on Christ, not on Satan or demons. A high view of God's righteousness and character, a clear view of Jesus' sinlessness, obedience, and sacrifice, and a balanced view of Satan are all imperative in discussing the paranormal. This is the way to keep balance and perspective.

What about those clever objections children and teens can come up with? The next chapter should help in responding to some of these objections.

17

RESPONDING TO
OBJECTIONS

*Magic is a game of strategy, using the "magic" theme as a
backbone to the game. It is not about devils and evil things.
Those are just names and different "flavors" of the game.*[1]

"But it works." "It's just a game." "The Bible has bad
stuff in it, too." These are all common objections you might
hear to restrictions you put on your kids' activities that
involve paranormal themes. But part of your job as a parent
is to set reasonable limits, depending on the age and matu-
rity of your child, and depending on your own beliefs based
on the Bible. This is a difficult and thankless task, and gray
areas make it harder.

But be encouraged because you have God's Word and
the Holy Spirit to guide you. God knows that we are not perfect, and he will provide the guidance and strength we need.

"BUT IT'S JUST A GAME."

I'll say it right up front: Don't confuse innocent fantasy and imagination with content that endorses spells or supernatural magic (or perhaps violence that you deem too extreme). Your guide for this should be the basic practices forbidden by God: divination, casting spells and doing magical rituals or acts, and spirit contact. Sometimes it takes time and discernment to discover what a game is about. So what do you do when you hear, "But it's only a game"?

When my son was eleven, he wanted to play a game that contained occult elements and I told him he could not. I kept presenting my reasons and he kept disagreeing (don't you think sometimes that your children would make great lawyers!). Finally, it hit me that, as the parent, I was answerable to God for how I was raising my son. Being a single parent, I pointed out to my son that I was the spiritual head of the household and would have to answer to God for my decisions regarding him. This sobered my son up instantly, and he dropped the argument and accepted my decision. You may not get the same result, but it's a good point to make anyway.

Sit down with your child and go over some of the passages that reveal God's attitude toward spells and occult magic, such as Deuteronomy 18:9–14. The suggestions in the "Bringing It Home" sections are meant to help you or give you some ideas in how to do this. Say that you realize that the game is *just a game*, but that you have reservations based on God's Word, and you would prefer your child not to be exposed to the terminology and ideas of paranormal magic and spells, or to games that depict supernatural magic as good. Explain that some people actually practice magic and spells for real. Make it clear that you realize this is not the actual practice of spells or magic (or spirit contact), but that your decision is based on the fact that the game makes these things seem good, or uses terms and actions you believe are unwholesome for your child's mind and spirit.

Your child might argue that the Bible also contains "bad things." Or your child might challenge that some of the things in the game you are questioning or forbidding are good. For example, Magic: The Gathering has cards that are neutral or promote what appear to be good characters.

These two objections are quite common. Here are a few points you can make to answer the objections. While some of these points apply specifically to Magic: The Gathering, they can be applied to any game that incorporates elements of the occult:

1. Show your child Bible passages such as Deuteronomy 18:9–14 and others that speak out against divination and spiritism.

2. Explain that what is put in the mind *does* matter, according to God (see Philippians 4:8).

3. Admit that the Bible gives accounts of many "bad" things and people, but that it does not *endorse* evil. Rather, the Bible clearly teaches against evil and how humans are redeemed from the penalty for sin through Christ. The stories of evil deeds in the Bible are a contrast to the holiness, grace, and mercy of God, and only amplify the grace of God available in the gift of salvation.

4. Just as you want to feed your child only good food, so you also want only good food for his or her mind and spirit. Tell your children that you are just as concerned about spiritual and emotional health as you are about physical health, and spiritual and emotional "food" is just as important to inspect as physical food.

5. Discuss the obvious contradiction that magic, spells, and sorcery are condemned by God, but in this game they are considered tools that can be used for good.

6. Explain that just because cards or characters in the game refer to good things, this does not make the game okay.

7. Discuss the influence of their behavior on others. If your child is into the playing-card games Magic: The Gathering or Yu-Gi-Oh, ask: "What might your decision to play these games say to the people you play (or trade cards) with? What roles should your example play in relating to others?" Read 1 Corinthians 8:9–12 and explain how this passage teaches the principle of avoiding behavior that causes a weaker person to stumble.

8. If your child is a believer, explain how Christians are to be salt and light in the world, and how engaging in some of these games might compromise this.

One good option to help minimize your child's potential disappointment in the restrictions you choose is to provide alternative books and games that promote a healthy use of imagination and fantasy. Chinese Checkers, Clue, Bridge, Backgammon, Monopoly, Risk, Scrabble, Trivial Pursuit games, and others offer plenty of fun without the occult content. Numerous new games (including computer and video games) based on the Bible or biblical themes are released every year. Chess, although it can be a complex strategy game, can be taught to children as young as six or seven, and is an excellent game for developing thinking and concentration skills.

"BUT IT WORKS."

Numerous kids have told me that they've witnessed paranormal activity at work—seeing something fly across the room after someone cast a spell, experiencing something "unusual" or "creepy" while playing with the Ouija board. Or they've heard stories about spells that "really worked" and believe them to be true. Teens at one youth group told me that a girl at school had put a spell on a teacher and that teacher got cancer.

Don't argue whether something supernatural happened or not (unless there is an obvious natural explanation, or you were there and witnessed the event and have a valid explanation). Whether it happened or not, your child may believe it did even if you argue against it (particularly if your argument is based on feelings or hearsay instead of facts). I prefer to use their account to make certain points.

I usually give these responses:

1. People who are doing spells or magic think they have a power or are getting power, but if something supernatural is really going on, they are not using the power, the power is using them.

2. The results from spells are often coincidences or things that would happen anyway. There is no way to prove spells work or do not work, but either way, they are to be avoided. When spells don't work, those who do spells have many explanations for the failure. In the case of the teacher getting cancer, I pointed out that in all likelihood the teacher may already have had the cancer when the spell was done, and if not, it was just a coincidence that the teacher got cancer. It is faulty logic to connect the cancer with the spell.

3. If there is a supernatural event, like an object flying across the room, compare that with the awesome power of God. He created a universe with so many galaxies and stars that astronomers can't even count them, and he created all of that from nothing! He knows the number of hairs on your head (see Matthew 10:30). God knows the past, present, and future of every person in the world who has lived, is living now, and ever will live. God knows everything going on all the time. Now, how great does it seem that some object flew across the room compared to what you know about God? Seems kind of puny, doesn't it?

4. Tarot cards are supposed to be kept inside a certain kind of box or wrapped in certain material, like silk. The tarot reader is not to let anyone else handle the cards (the latter is also true for magical tools). This supposedly protects the cards from "negative energy" that might cause the reading to go awry. Witches must cast a circle a certain way and cannot allow anyone or anything to "break" the circle or the magic is messed up. "Well," I like to ask kids, "what kind of power is this? Sounds kind of delicate to me. Do Christians need to worry that God won't hear them if they don't pray in a certain position or say certain words? Do Bibles need to be wrapped in silk cloth or kept in a wooden box when not being read? Will a Bible lose its value if it sits on a table or bookshelf?" This is a humorous and pointed way to show the bondage that comes from the occult and how free we are as believers in Christ from such complicated and intricate requirements.

QUESTIONS ABOUT MIRACLES AND SUPERNATURAL POWER

One of the most common questions, from both Christians and non-Christians, is about the differences between biblical miracles and what seem to be supernatural powers in the occult. Some people believe that psychic powers, for example, are the same as the abilities possessed by biblical prophets, with the difference being that the prophets used their "abilities" for God.

There is no biblical evidence that the prophets had their own special powers or abilities; on the contrary, God gave them direct revelation. The prophets did not initiate visions or revelation through techniques, nor did they claim special talents of their own. Rather, it was the Lord who chose them as his prophets and it was he who gave them direct revelation. The prophets prayed for answers or guidance from God, but they did not seek to instigate visions or revelation. They waited on God and on his timing.

Prophecies were not always about the future, but were also God's Word to people in the form of instruction, rebuke, comfort, or exhortation. Additionally, the prophets' revelations glorified God. These foretellings differ drastically from psychics' predictions about one's romance, job, money, or sundry personal situations.

The miracles performed both by Old Testament prophets and by Jesus glorified God. The miracles of Jesus fulfilled prophecies that the Messiah would heal the sick, make the blind see and the lame walk, and were a sign to show Jesus was the Messiah (see Isaiah 61:1–2; Matthew 11:2–5; and Luke 4:18–19). The apostles' ability to perform miracles was a sign that they were true followers of Jesus Christ.

Here are some differences between biblical miracles and

magical powers, according to noted apologist and theolo-
gian Norman L. Geisler:[2]

BIBLICAL MIRACLE	MAGICAL POWERS
Under God's control	Under man's control
Done at God's will	Done at human's will
Supernatural	Supernatural seen as natural
Associated with good	Can be good or bad
Can overcome evil	Cannot overpower God
To affirm Jesus as God	To deny Jesus as God
Prophecies always correct	Prophecies have error
Never associated with the occult	Associated with occult techniques

ASK ABOUT SCHOOL AND FRIENDS

Christian parents need to ask their kids (especially those in
seventh grade and above) if there are any Wiccans, witches,
or others who claim to do magic in their schools. You might
be surprised to discover that your children have schoolmates
who are involved in the occult.

In 2005, I gave a talk to a large youth group and asked
the kids to raise their hands if there were Wiccans in their
schools. Several kids raised their hands, and I went on to
talk about Wicca. After the talk, I found out that two of the

adult youth workers did not even know what Wicca was. So it is to your advantage as parents (or as a worker with children or teens) to be informed and ask about your children's classmates.

Children who attend school with Wiccans or with kids who claim to do magic may worry about whether these kids can cast a spell against them. The best answer for this is to reassure them about God's power and being safe in Christ, and give them verses about trusting the Lord.

Sometimes it is difficult or upsetting for parents to think about all the bad stuff out in the world that is out to "get" our kids. Strive to be realistic without being fearful, cautious without being smothering, so that your children can eventually learn how to handle these challenges on their own. What steps can parents take to protect kids and equip them at the same time? That is coming up in the next and final chapter.

18

PROTECTING AND
EQUIPPING YOUR KIDS

For our struggle is not against flesh and blood, but against the rulers, against the powers, against the world forces of this darkness, against the spiritual forces of wickedness in the heavenly places. (Ephesians 6:12)

No temptation has overtaken you but such as is common to man; and God is faithful, who will not allow you to be tempted beyond what you are able, but with the temptation will provide the way of escape also, so that you will be able to endure it. (1 Corinthians 10:13)

W hen your child was young, no doubt you warned him or her about talking to strangers. You were probably constantly on guard. As children get older, the way you

227

protect them changes—it becomes more complex and difficult. It's not unusual to wonder if you are making the right decisions. Naturally, prayer for your children is essential. Pray for their protection, and that they would have wisdom and discernment. Teach them to pray for these things, and let them know you pray for them.

It is helpful for children to know that Satan is a tempter who seeks to pull believers away from their walk with Christ. Although still accountable for choices and actions, Christians can resist temptation in the strength of Christ, and ask forgiveness if they stumble. There is no need for kids to continue to feel guilty about something they've asked forgiveness for.

INTERNET DARTS

Many experts advise parents to locate the computer in a common area like the kitchen, den, or living room so that parents can better monitor their children on the Internet.

Filters for porn on computers will do nothing to prevent kids from finding Web sites with occult material, nor will filters keep them from engaging with others via chat rooms, e-mail discussions, or IM (instant messaging). There is no need for paranoia, but these conversations can be potent darts of the enemy that attack your child's faith or even attempt to recruit your child to another worldview.

Many involved in the occult or in pagan religions are skilled in tactics that appear to undermine Scripture and present an appealing view of *their* beliefs. In many cases this is not done maliciously. Most probably think they are viewing things correctly and are simply freeing a child or teen from narrow-minded views or rescuing them from the clutches of hypocritical religion. Dealing with such assaults on faith is difficult even for Christian adults, and it is certainly beyond the abilities of children and most teens.

Train yourself and your child in how to respond to some of the more common attacks on the faith, such as the claim that the Bible has contradictions, because eventually your child will confront this.[1]

THE RELIGIOUS DISGUISE OF THE OCCULT

Let your child know that Satan disguises himself as an angel of light (see 2 Corinthians 11:14), and that people, beliefs, and practices that appear to be good or even Christian may actually be *opposed* to Christianity. The occult freely borrows from the Bible, and many psychics, astrologers, card readers, and others speak of knowing God and may claim to be Christian. It is up to you to teach your child that what anyone says needs to be taken in context with what the person is doing. No matter what the person says he or she believes, if what the person is teaching or doing goes against God's Word, the teachings and practices are to be rejected. While you don't want to make your child paranoid, you do need to teach your child how to be discerning, and that the Bible tells us to be vigilant.

IT'S A GOOD THING TO THINK

A lot of messages permeate the culture and emphasize feeling over thinking, the nonrational over the rational, one's experience as truth, and subjective data over the objective. This is fallout from New Age and postmodern thinking and it feeds a natural selfish desire to give priority to feelings and experiences. Since the world of the occult emphasizes the subjective and intuitive over objective facts or rational thinking, here are some things you can teach your children to help immunize them from falling into these traps:

- God is objectively true; Christ the Savior is the Way, the Truth, and the Life (see John 14:6)[2]; and God's Word is truth (see John 10:35; 17:17; Colossians 1:5; 2 Peter 1:20), so all teachings should be measured by these objective truths.

- Experiences and subjective feelings are normal and fine, but they are not the way we decide what is true; feelings can be misleading and deceptive (see Jeremiah 17:9).

- The Bible itself is written in words, and words themselves are based on logical, rational order. The mind must be engaged for us to read and understand God's Word. Reason and logic are based in God's character; God is not a God of confusion (see 1 Corinthians 14:33).

- We are told to love God with all our heart, soul, and *mind* (see Matthew 22:37; Mark 12:30; Luke 20:27).

- Although humans sometimes put their wisdom above God's, this flaw does not negate the value of thoughtful evaluation of ideas and teachings. The Bible endorses reason, sound judgment, and rational thinking (see Isaiah 1:18; Psalm 119:59; Matthew 22:37; Acts 17:2, 17; 18:4, 19; 19:8;

Romans 12:3; 1 Corinthians 14; Philippians 4:8; 1 Peter 4:7).

Teach your child to be wary of any instruction that places feelings over thinking, or promotes the belief that logic and reason are negative. You will help inoculate your child against many New Age and occult beliefs that counter God's truth.

THE ARMOR OF GOD

Ephesians 6, starting with verse 10, tells us to put on the armor of God. The armor of a soldier is used as a metaphor, indicating that this is about being equipped for spiritual war. This is not sensational material. Scripture is speaking clearly and calmly on this topic.

Why put on the armor? Verse 11 says it is so believers can "stand firm against the schemes of the devil." Verse 12 states that "our struggle is not against flesh and blood," and reveals that this is not about physical attack, but rather a spiritual war waged by Satan and his minions. Satan takes an active role in attacking and attempting to undermine Christians through his "schemes." Verses 11, 13, and 14 all admonish us to "stand firm." That this phrase is repeated three times shows its significance. This is not about going forth to conquer, but is rather about resistance and standing firm within the armor.

The pieces of armor—the girding of loins (some translations use "belt"), the breastplate, the shodding of feet, the shield, the helmet, and the sword—illustrate the accompanying principles in which we are to abide: truth, righteousness, the gospel of peace, faith, salvation, and the Word of the

Lord. In other words, believers in Christ are to be grounded in these six truths of the faith, truths that are immovable and indestructible. Can anything defeat the Lord's truth, right-eousness, peace, faith, salvation, and Word? Wearing this armor means being grounded in what is unerring and unshakable. Christians cannot stand alone and unprotected, which is why we need this armor.

Investigate together other Bible passages, especially those in the Old Testament, that relate to the Ephesians armor. Girding our loins with righteousness and faithfulness can be found in Isaiah 11:5 where the coming Messiah is described. The breastplate of righteousness and the helmet of salvation are found in Isaiah 59:17, a passage where God intervenes to bring justice. A New Testament passage, 1 Thessalonians 5:8, urges us to be "sober" and put on "the breastplate of faith and love, and as a helmet, the hope of salvation."

The reference to feet shod with the gospel of peace takes us to Isaiah 52:7, a poetic passage describing a mes-senger who brings peace and good news, announcing God's future redemption of Israel. Romans 10:15 refers to the same Isaiah passage in speaking of how the good news of the gospel is spread.

One of the most vivid images is the portrayal of God's Word as a sword. The word for "sword" in verse 17 is *machaira*, which was a short but very sharp two-edged sword, and is the only offensive weapon listed. This is the same word in Hebrews 4:12, which expresses God's Word as being "sharper than any two-edged sword." Think of how Jesus responded with Scripture to Satan's temptations in the wilderness!

Look up and discuss with your child other Bible pas-sages that depict God's Word as a sword, such as Isaiah 49:2, Hosea 6:5, and especially those in connection with Jesus in Revelation 1:16; 2:12, 16; 19:15 and 21, where a "sharp, two-edged sword" comes out of the mouth of Jesus. This striking imagery will make an impact on a child and is something that a child can easily imagine and remember.

The last part of the passage urges prayer "at all times in the Spirit" and to be on the alert (Ephesians 6:18). Other New Testament passages urge believers to be alert and sober, such as 1 Peter 1:13: "Therefore, prepare your minds for action, keep sober in spirit, fix your hope completely on the grace to be brought to you at the revelation of Jesus Christ."

Additional confirmation that the believer's weapons in this spiritual warfare are spiritual is in 2 Corinthians 10:3–4: "For though we walk in the flesh, we do not war according to the flesh, for the weapons of our warfare are not of the flesh, but divinely powerful for the destruction of fortresses." The passage continues in verse 5, exhorting believers to bring "every thought captive to the obedience of Christ."

The key to this warfare is in James 4:7, where we are instructed to "submit therefore to God. Resist the devil, and he will flee from you." The crucial element is submission to God, which is enhanced by daily walking with the Lord, reading and studying his Word, prayer, worshipping him, and seeking his will. This is the stuff that Satan fears and hates.

ALWAYS A WAY OUT

Encourage your children to understand that, although they will face temptations in this area, God always gives us a way out. Teach your child 1 Corinthians 10:13, in which God promises us that there is no trial or temptation that we cannot bear, and that he provides a way out.

Teaching your children that sometimes believers must take unpopular stands will help prepare them to do this as they grow older and eventually move from home. If your child is at a sleepover and the other kids get out a Ouija board, he or she can politely decline to participate and can silently pray instead. (I have talked with children and teens who have done this. In one case, after one child prayed, the planchette on the Ouija board did not move and the kids gave up on it.) If your child is confident, he or she might even be willing to say something to deter the other kids from using the board, but I would not pressure a child into thinking he or she must do this.

When my son was in the fifth grade, some kids at lunch were talking about a Ouija board they had made in the after-school program, and how a pencil had flown across the room during their session with the board. My son, who was a fairly new believer at the time, made a remark that the Ouija board was evil, and most of the kids laughed. Your children may get laughed at, but when they have been prepared at home on the importance of standing strong in their faith, and if they are taught biblical principles, they will handle this derision with grace. Most kids are pretty resilient, and learning to take a stand on certain things when they are younger will help them later when even more difficult temptations come along.

PERSISTENT PRAYER PLEASES GOD

While on Earth, Jesus prayed to his Father regularly. He often went off alone to pray to the Father. In Luke 18:1–8,

Jesus tells the parable of the widow whose persistence in petitioning the "unrighteous" judge *"who did not fear God and did not respect man"* finally pays off when the judge grants her relief. Verse 1 states that Jesus tells this story *"to show that at all times they ought to pray and not to lose heart."*

Other passages to ponder on prayer are Colossians 4:2, *"Devote yourselves to prayer, keeping alert in it with an attitude of thanksgiving,"* and 1 Thessalonians 5:17, *"Pray without ceasing."* Teaching your children these passages will encourage them to pray and help them realize that God values prayer.

Training children in regular prayer is essential. Prayer is not a system to get what we want, but a path to grow the desire to be in God's will. God will work through prayers. Pray for your child's protection and discernment. Teach your child to pray for wisdom and to stay strong in Christ.

Encourage your children to pray for any child they might know who is involved in the occult. Such prayer is not only to ask God to work in the lives of the unbelievers, but prayer itself alters the petitioner from the inside out, stimulating compassion and allowing Christians to see others through God's eyes.

Concluding Words

*M*y hope and prayer is that this book has edified and empowered you in the very difficult area of the paranormal and occult. Too many Christians have avoided learning about this area because it is difficult to get sound information and it can be intimidating. You don't need to be a student of the occult to teach your children how to respond to it, but it is helpful to understand overarching principles in order to recognize it, and then assess the situation through the filter of God's Word.

Tread lightly but firmly, always rooted in God's Word, when dealing with these topics. Christians should be neither frightened nor apathetic about the paranormal. Rather, we should look to God's Word and be discerning and prepared for the sake of our children.

NOTES

1: WHAT IS THE PARANORMAL? THE HIDDEN AND FORBIDDEN

1. R. Laird Harris, ed., *Theological Wordbook of the Old Testament, Vol. II* (Chicago: Moody Press, 1980), 80 (hereafter abbreviated as TWOT).
2. Ibid., 685.
3. Merrill F. Unger, *The New Unger's Bible Dictionary*, edited by R. K. Harrison (Chicago: Moody Press, 1988), 802.
4. "Lexical Aids to the Old Testament," *The Hebrew-Greek Key Study Bible*, edited by Spiros Zodhiates (AMG, 1990), 1705, 1737; Unger, 803.

2: HIDDEN MEANINGS, HIDDEN POWERS, HIDDEN BEINGS

1. S. W., fifteen-year-old practitioner of ceremonial magic, in undated e-mail to author.
2. E-mails to author, June 24 and June 26, 2002.
3. *The New Encyclopaedia Britannica*, 15th ed., s.v. "Occultism." (Chicago), 85.
4. The term *magick*, when being used as an occult practice is sometimes spelled with a *k* to distinguish it from stage magic, which is done using tricks. The spelling "magic" will be used in this book unless it is a quote, and will refer to real magic, not stage magic, unless otherwise noted.
5. Deva is a word also used in Hinduism and Theosophy and takes on somewhat different meanings in those contexts.
6. William S. Lyon, "Working with Sacred Power," *Shaman's Drum*, Mid-Spring, 1989, no. 16, 39; "The distinguishing characteristic of shamanism is its focus on an ecstatic trance state in which the soul of the shaman is believed to leave the body and ascend to the sky (heavens) or descend into the earth (underworld)," Dean Edwards, "What is Shamanism?" http://www.deoxy.org/shaover.htm#2.
7. *Merriam-Webster Online Dictionary* defines "incantation" as "a use of spells or verbal charms spoken or sung as a part of a ritual of magic; *also*: a written or recited formula of words designed to produce a particular effect." http://www.m-w.com/cgi-bin/dictionary?book=Dictionary&va=incantation.
8. Unger, 1319.
9. Persephone, e-mail to author, August 11, 2005.
10. Rachel Pollack, *Teach Yourself Fortunetelling* (New York: Holt, 1986), 14.
11. Phyllis Galde, *The Truth About Crystal Healing* (St. Paul, MN: Llewellyn, 1994), 26.
12. Shamanism is usually found as part of animistic religions that incorporate contacting spirits as a regular practice. Shamans employ occult methods, such as sorcery, spirit contact, going into trances, and reading omens.

13. Donald Michael Kraig, *The Truth About Psychic Powers* (St. Paul, MN: Llewellyn, 1994), 19.

14. Ibid., 18.

3: Fantasy vs. the Paranormal

1. M. S., e-mail to author, September 6, 2002.

4: Bewitching Entertainment

1. http://www.scholastic.com/titles/twitches/magickarchive.htm.

2. E-mail to author from fifteen-year-old practitioner of ritual magic, undated.

3. Llewellyn's *New Worlds of Mind and Spirit*, Sept/Oct 1996, 6.

4. Melissa Wickham, "Teen Witch Caught Up in Spells," *Nation News*, June 26, 2005. http://www.nationnews.com/story/296175434721804.php.

5. Silver Ravenwolf, *Teen Witch* (St. Paul, MN: Llewellyn, 1998).

6. Silver Ravenwolf, *Angels: Companions in Magick* (St. Paul, MN: Llewellyn, 1996).

7. Karen MacPherson, "Book Trend Casts Spell Over Young Readers," *Pittsburgh Post-Gazette*, July 31, 2001, http://www.post-gazette.com/ae/20010731witchbooks0731p3.asp.

8. Ibid.

9. Michael Kress, "Bewitching Readers With Pagan Lore," *Publisher's Weekly*, June 14, 1999, 24–26.

10. Judith Rosen, "Casting a Wider Spell," *Publisher's Weekly*, September 1, 2003, http://publishersweekly.reviewsnews.com/index.asp?layout=article&articleid=CA319870&publication=publishersweekly.

11. Erin Hartigan, "Conjuring a Feast to Welcome Back Harry," *Washington Post*, July 5, 2005, F6.

12. http://tv.disney.go.com/jetix/witch/index.html.

13. http://www.scholastic.com/titles/twitches/magickarchive.htm.

14. http://www.scholastic.com/titles/twitches/magick.asp.

5: THE DARK SIDE

1. S. W., undated e-mail to author.

2. Jean Yolen, *Wizardry Hall* (New York: Magic Carpet Books/Harcourt, 1999), 83.

3. D. Howard Smith, *The Wisdom of the Taoists* (New York: New Directions, 1980), 42.

4. Georg Feuerstein, *Spirituality by the Numbers* (New York: Tarcher, 1994), 146.

5. From the *Chuang Tzu* as quoted in Geoffrey Parrinder, ed., *World Religions: From Ancient History to the Present* (New York: Facts on File, 1983), 333.

6. Wen-Tzu, *Further Teachings of Lao-Tzu* (Boston: Shambhala, 1992), 109.

7. Jan and Stewart Farrar, "The Wiccan Path," *A Witches' Bible: The Complete Witches' Handbook* (Custer, WA: Phoenix Publishing, 1996), 107.

8. Persephone, e-mail to author, August 11, 2005.

9. John J. Coughlin, "Reclaiming Darkness in Paganism: A Call to Balance," http://www.waningmoon.com/darkpagan/lib/lib0046.shtml.

10. Rabbi David A. Cooper, *God Is a Verb* (New York: Riverhead Books/Penguin Putnam, 1997), 155.

11. Ibid., 156.

12. Ibid., 160.

13. Deepak Chopra, *How to Know God* (New York: Harmony Books/Random House, 2000), 170.

14. Arthur Edward Waite, *The Book of Ceremonial Magick* (New York: Citatdel Press Book/Carol Publishing Group, 1994), xxiv.

15. "Leviathan," e-mail to author, July 27, 2005.

16. See http://www.adherents.com/people/pl/George_Lucas.html: "Lucas was born and raised in a strongly Methodist family. After

inserting religious themes into *Star Wars* he would eventually come to identify strongly with the Eastern religious philosophies he studied and incorporated into his movies, which were a major inspiration for 'the Force.' Lucas eventually came to state that his religion was 'Buddhist Methodist.' Gary Kurtz, a Latter-day Saint who had studied Comparative Religion extensively in college and on his own, was pivotal in introducing Lucas to Eastern religions (particularly Buddhism) and Native American religion, and discussing with Lucas how best to improve 'Star Wars' by giving it a believable but sufficiently universal religious underpinning. Kurtz was the producer of 'Star Wars' and 'The Empire Strikes Back' and also did some work on the 'Star Wars' screenplay." Also see Norman L. Geisler and J. Yutaka Amano, *Religion of the Force* (Dallas: Quest, 1983), and "The Star Wars Religion" at http://sw-anthropo.ibelgique.com/txt/religiontxtangl.html.

17. Wickham.

6: WHAT'S YOUR SIGN? THE MYSTIQUE AND MISTAKE OF ASTROLOGY

1. http://www.walmart.com/catalog/product.gsp?product_id=3287844.
2. http://www.walmart.com/catalog/product.gsp?product_id=3287844#long_descr.
3. Karma is the law of action; in Hindu thinking, whatever action you take will lead to a result for you, good or bad, in your next life or in some future life.
4. Reincarnation, found in Hinduism and some forms of Buddhism, is the belief that everyone who dies returns after death in another human body to live out another life.
5. The "spiritual master" was a spirit being, often called a spirit guide, who was presented as an advanced spiritual teacher from a higher realm or level. Guided visualization is a technique that puts one into an altered state or mild hypnotic trance through a relaxation exercise, specified breathing patterns, and directing the

person to imagine certain things at certain points of the process.

6. Unger, 798–99.

7. Merrill C. Tenney and Steven Barabas, eds., *The Zondervan Pictorial Encyclopedia of the Bible* (Grand Rapids: Zondervan, 1975), vol. 4, 31; Gregory W. Bromiley, *Theological Dictionary of the New Testament* (Grand Rapids: Eerdmans and Paternoster, 1985), 547.

8. John Ankerberg, John Weldon, "Astrology and Spiritism," http://64.233.161.104/search?q=cache:9sh7pw5vTokJ: www.ankerberg.com/Articles/_PDFArchives/new-age/ NA1W0601.pdf+charles+strohmer+astrology&hl=en.

9. Strohmer, quoted in Ankerberg.

7: WHO ARE THE PSYCHICS AND CAN THEY HELP?

1. C. G., e-mail to author, June 25, 2005.

2. John McCrone, "Exploding the ten percent myth" http://www.sci-con.org/articles/20040901.html.

3. Benjamin Radford, "The Ten Percent Myth," *Skeptical Inquirer*, March/April 1999, http://www.sci-con.org/articles/20040901.html; Eric Chudler, "Myths About the Brain: 10 Percent and Counting," http://www.brainconnection.com/topics/?main=fa/brain-myth; "Do We Use Only 10% of Our Brain?" http://faculty.washington.edu/chudler/tenper.html.

4. Migene Gonzalez-Whippler, *The Complete Book of Spells, Ceremonies & Magic* (St. Paul: Llewellyn, 1996), 99.

5. Reincarnation is the belief that all of us come back after death in another body and that this cycle repeats itself for a long time until the point where we are spiritually advanced enough to leave Earth permanently.

6. Belief that Christ achieved a higher consciousness through realizing his innate divinity, and that we all have this innate divinity and can achieve the same realization.

7. The term *Spirit* is often used by those in the New Age or occult to refer to the kind of God they may believe in, to a universal

type of spirit that we are all a part of, or to an energy or force that connects us all. Various spiritual views are found among psychics, so no one view can be given, though the views are often similar. It is not uncommon for this term to be used with no precise meaning being implied by it.

8. Books such as *A Course in Miracles* and *The Aquarian Gospel* are claimed to have been "channeled"—given to someone who was channeling a spirit and written down by that person. Many claim to channel aliens or spirits from another dimension, and these teachings are not unusual in New Age and alien/UFO-oriented literature.

9. Parapsychological Association Web page, http://www.parapsych.org/.

10. Julie Tallard Johnson, *Teen Psychic: Exploring Your Intuitive Spiritual Powers* (Rochester, VT: Bindu Books, 2003). The information here was adapted from my review of this book published in the *Christian Research Journal*, vol. 28, no. 1, 48–49.

11. Ibid., 177–79.

12. Ibid., 197.

13. Carole Braden, "Real-life 'mediums,'" *Good Housekeeping*, November, 2005, 124.

14. Ibid.

15. Ibid., 127.

8: DIVINATION—NOT DIVINE!

1. Unger, 802–3.

2. "Numerology—Gematria: The Mathematics of the Torah," http://www.inner.org/gematria/gematria.htm.

3. "Foretelling the Future by the Numbers: An Introduction to Arithmancy, by Hermione Granger," http://www.wizarding wireless.net/wwn.arithmancy.html © David Haber.

4. Unger, 803.

5. Richard Simon, ed., *Beyond Psychology*, Networker U Resource Catalogue (EEG Spectrum International, Inc., 2004), 19. The

catalogue offered descriptions of courses for the "Psychotherapy Networker Symposium," March 17–20, 2005, Washington, D.C.

6. Joey Korn, "Dowsing: A Path to Enlightenment," *Magical Blend*, August 2005, 9.

7. Tatiana Elmanovich, "Ruth Montgomery: A Conversation in Naples, Florida on April 2, 2000," http://www.tanika.com/04-Mediums/ruth.htm.

8. Neale Donald Walsch, *Conversations with God: An Uncommon Dialogue, Book 1* (New York: Putnam, 1996), 1.

9. This paragraph was taken from the author's article, "Conversations with God for Teens: Don't Talk to Strangers," first published in *Midwest Christian Outreach Journal*, vol. 9, no. 1, Winter/Spring 2003. This article is online at http://cana.userworld.com/cana_ConvWGodTeens_adults.html.

10. Rosemary Guiley, *Harper's Encyclopedia of Mystical and Paranormal Experience* (Edison, NJ: Castle Books, 1991), 502; Eden Gray, *A Complete Guide to the Tarot* (New York: Bantam/Crown, 1972), 6; Lewis Spence, *An Encyclopedia of Occultism* (Carol Publishing Group Edition, 1996; New York: Citadel Press, 1988), 403.

11. Guiley, *Harper's*, 602.

12. Ibid., 603; Gray, 14.

13. Gray, 2.

14. Ibid.

15. Ibid., 12, 14; Spence, 403.

16. Guiley, *Harper's*, 603.

17. Gray, 14.

18. "What is Palm Reading?" http://articles.syl.com/whatispalmreading.html.

19. Guiley, *Harper's*, 424.

20. Spence, 409.

21. Donald Tyson, *The Truth About Runes* (St. Paul: Llewellyn, 1995), 19.

22. *Twist*, December 1998, 50.

23. Belinda Henwood with Consultant Howard Choy, *Feng Shui* (Pownal, VT: Storey Books, undated), 8, 12; Lillian Too, *The*

Complete Illustrated Guide to Feng Shui (Boston: Element Books Inc., 1996), 74; Eva Wong, *The Shambhala Guide to Taoism* (Boston: Shambhala Publications, Inc., 1997), 126, 133.
24. Guiley, *Harper's*, 279.
25. Ibid., 279–80.

9: Is Magic Just in Fairy Tales? Part One

1. E-mail message to author, December 15, 2004.
2. Amaranth, e-mail message to author, August 24, 2001.
3. *Merriam-Webster Online Dictionary,* http://www.m-w.com/ cgi-bin/dictionary?book=Dictionary&va=sorcery.
4. Allan Zola Kronzck and Elizabeth Kronzck, *The Sorcerer's Companion: A Guide to the Magical World of Harry Potter* (New York: Broadway Books, 2001), 208–210.
5. Ibid., 210.
6. *Merriam-Webster Online Dictionary,* http://www.m-w.com/cgi-bin/dictionary?book=Dictionary&va=magic+.
7. Ibid.
8. Arthur Edward Waite, *The Book of Ceremonial Magic* (New York: Citadel Press Book, Carol Publishing Group Edition, 1994; University Books, Inc., 1989), XL.

10: Is Magic Just in Fairy Tales? Part Two

1. Anonymous, e-mail to author, June 24, 2002.
2. Gerald and Betty Schueler, *Enochian Magick* (St. Paul: Llewellyn, 1996), 1; Anton and Mina Adams, *The World of Wizards* (New York: Metro Books, 2002), 30. This definition comes from the notorious and controversial ritual magician Aleister Crowley. The book by the Adamses was one of many books on magic that came out when the Harry Potter series was garnering so much publicity.

3. J. H. Brennan, *Magick for Beginners: The Power to Change Your World* (St. Paul: Llewellyn, 1999), 5. This book was given to me by a fourteen-year-old girl in a youth group after I talked to the group and to her privately about the dangers of the occult.

4. Guiley, *Harper's*, 336.

5. "Kabbalah" may be spelled several ways, but normally when it is being used for occult practices—something many Kabbalists disavow and denounce—it is spelled "Qabalah" or a variation thereof.

6. Guiley, *Harper's*, 336. Concepts of the "Divine" vary, but may include a view of a remote god, and that one must practice magical rituals or follow esoteric teachings in order to purify one's self and thus please and return to or have union with this god. The term *the divine* is often used by occultists and Pagans.

7. From chapter 2, the definition of visualization: "Visualization is a method for picturing a desired goal clearly in the mind and believing it is already accomplished in order to bring it into reality."

8. Brennan, 45.

9. Donald Tyson, *The Truth About Ritual Magic* (St. Paul: Llewellyn, 1989; 2nd ed. 1994), 29.

10. Donald Michael Kraig, *Evocation of Spirits* (St. Paul: Llewellyn, 1994), 2.

11. Ibid., 37; Brennan, 18–19; Waite; throughout the book, God and Jesus are called upon and addressed in various prayers and incantations.

12. Adams, *The World of Wizards*, 11.

13. Tyson, *Runes*, 3.

14. Guiley, *Encyclopedia of Witches and Witchcraft* (New York: Facts on File/Checkmark Books, 1999), 310.

15. Ravenwolf, *Angels*, 199.

16. Ibid., 111–12.

17. Tyson, *Runes*, 5.

18. Tyson, *Runes*, 6, 25.

19. Some of this information is from Guiley, *Harper's*, 16–17.

20. Guiley, *Witches and Witchcraft*, 327.

21. Guiley, *Harper's*, 599–600.
22. Silver Ravenwolf, "What Do You Mean, Your Spells Don't Work?" in *Llewellyn's 1995 Magical Almanac* (St. Paul: Llewellyn, 1994), 216.
23. Guiley, *Witches and Witchcraft*, 316.
24. Jan and Stewart Farrar, "Leaves From the Book of Shadows," in *A Witches' Bible: The Complete Witches' Handbook* (Custer, WA: Phoenix Publishing, 1984), 235.
25. Gerina Dunwich, *Wicca Craft* (New York: Citadel Press, 1991; Carol Publishing Group Edition, 1994), 86.
26. *Spirit* is undefined or defined loosely but seems to refer to a sacred energy or consciousness permeating creation.
27. TWOT, 259–60.
28. Brennan, 3.
29. Tyson, *Ritual Magic*, 19–20.
30. Adams, *The Learned Arts of Witches and Wizards*, 6.

11: Magic as a Game

1. "The Altar and Its Tools," http://www.fortunecity.com/greenfield/tigris/567/id34.htm.
2. Jack, e-mail to author, April 17, 2002.
3. Richard Baker, *Advanced Dungeons & Dragons Rulebook, PLAYER'S OPTION: Spells & Magic* (Lake Geneva, WI: TSR, 1996), 12.
4. Tony Nixon, "Wizards of Dusk & Gloom," *Dragon Magazine*, Issue #261, Vol. XXIV, No. 2, July 1999, 29.
5. Ibid.
6. Ibid., 30–31.
7. *Dragon Magazine*, Issue #252, Vol. XXIII, No. 5, October 1998.
8. Ibid., Anne Brown, "101 Hauntings," 44–45.
9. Baker, 10.
10. Ibid., 13.
11. Ibid., 85.

12. Ibid., 90–91.

13. The *Washington Post*, Weekend Section, May 27, 1995, 13.

14. Rich Redman and Eric Doohan, "Introduction," in *Magic the Gathering: The Pocket Players' Guide* (Wizards of the Coast, 1995), ix.

15. Ibid., B-75.

16. Jeff Gomez, *Magic the Gathering Wayfarer* (New York: Acclaim Comics, no date).

17. Ibid.

18. http://www.albertweb.com/evenachild/editorials/yugioh.html.

19. http://www.gamespot.com/gbc/puzzle/yugiohdarkduelstories/review.html.

20. http://www.upperdeckentertainment.com/yugioh/en/products.aspx.

21. http://www.upperdeckentertainment.com/yugioh/en/check lists.aspx?checklist=yugi_deck&pdf=sdy.

22. http://www.upperdeckentertainment.com/yugioh/en/check lists.aspx?checklist=booster08&pdf=mfc.

23. http://www.upperdeckentertainment.com/yugioh/en/check lists.aspx?checklist=booster11&pdf=ast.

24. Rhonda Handlon, "Yu-Gi-Oh! The Movie," PluggedIn.Online, http://www.pluggedinonline.com/movies/movies/a0001856.cfm.

25. Ari Marmell, Dean Shomshak, and C. A. Suleiman, *Vampire: The Requiem* (Stone Mountain, GA: White Wolf, 2004; inspired by *Vampire: The Masquerade*, created by Mark Rein), 70.

26. World of Warcraft: Reign of Chaos, "Races of Azeroth," http://www.blizzard.com/war3/races/.

27. "Heroes," http://www.battle.net/war3/faq/heroes.shtml.

28. http://www.battle.net/war3/human/units/sorceress.shtml.

29. http://www.battle.net/war3/orc/units/farseer.shtml.

30. Lamar, in private message to author, July 13, 2005.

12: ANGELS OF LIGHT: DECEPTION FROM BEYOND
PART ONE

1. Anonymous e-mail to author, September 7, 2003.
2. Ravenwolf, *Angels*, x. This book is written to teens.
3. Ibid., 4.
4. Some of the information in this chapter was adapted from my article, "I See Dead People: A Look at After-Death Communication," *Christian Research Journal*, vol. 25, no. 01, 2002.
5. http://www.cbs.com/primetime/ghost_whisperer/blog.php
6. *A Course in Miracles* (Glen Allen, CA: Foundation for Inner Peace, 1992), 105.
7. Ibid., 527.
8. Ibid., xiii.
9. Ibid., 8–9, 281.
10. Marianne Williamson, *A Return to Love* (New York: HarperCollins Publishers, 1992), 29.
11. Jane Roberts, *The Nature of Personal Reality* (New York: Bantam Books, 1974), 157.
12. Ibid., 159; Williamson, 28; Neale Donald Walsch, *Conversations with God* (New York: G.P. Putnam's Sons, 1995), 52, 85.
13. John Edward, *One Last Time* paperback ed., (New York: Berkley, October 1999), 25–26. I was introduced to my spirit guide in a guided visualization in the mid-1970s. This is a technique whereby someone verbally guides a person into a meditative trance state through relaxation techniques and a series of suggested images; may also be called "guided imagery."
14. Edward, 43–45.
15. Ibid., 104.
16. Ibid., 109.
17. Ibid., 45, 107, 222.
18. Sylvia Browne, with Lindsay Harrison, *The Other Side and Back* (New York: Signet, 2000), xxiii, xxv.
19. Ibid., xxv.
20. Sylvia Browne, *Journey of the Soul Series, Book 1: God, Creation, and Tools for Life* (Carlsbad, CA: Hay House, 2000), 3.

21. Ibid., 22, 39.
22. Ibid., 185.
23. Browne, *The Other Side and Back*, 7, 13, 203; Browne, *God, Creation, and Tools for Life*, 7, 81.
24. Browne, *The Other Side and Back*, 181; Browne, *God, Creation, and Tools for Life*, 21, 150.
25. Browne, *God, Creation, and Tools for Life*, 4.
26. Ibid., 50, 74.
27. Browne, *The Other Side and Back*, 64.
28. Ibid., 3; Browne, *God, Creation, and Tools for Life*, 119.
29. Browne, *The Other Side and Back*, 4–5.
30. Ibid., 8–9, 216.
31. James Van Praagh, *Talking to Heaven: A Medium's Message of Life After Death* (New York: Signet, 1997), 4–5.
32. James Van Praagh, *Reaching to Heaven* (New York: Signet/New American Library, 1999), 26.
33. Van Praagh, *Talking to Heaven*, 8–9.
34. Ibid., 9–10.
35. Ibid., 29–30.
36. Ibid., 33.
37. Ibid., 34–37, 243.
38. Ibid., 41.
39. Ibid., 42.
40. Ibid., 43.
41. Van Praagh, *Reaching to Heaven*, 51–52, 92–93.
42. Van Praagh, *Talking to Heaven*, 40, 54–55.
43. Ibid., 55–56.
44. Tim Goodman, "Medium's Well-Done Show Wins Over Some Skeptics, Chats with the Dead Make Compelling TV," *San Francisco Chronicle*, January 23, 2001, http://www.sfgate.com/cgi-bin/article.cgi?file=/chronicle/archive/2001/01/23/DD26094.DTL; Browne, *The Other Side and Back*, xxiii, 58, 209; Van Praagh, *Reaching to Heaven*, 39.
45. Browne, *The Other Side and Back*, 58.
46. Edward, 43–52.
47. Goodman.
48. Browne, *The Other Side and Back*, 166.

13: ANGELS OF LIGHT: DECEPTION FROM BEYOND
PART TWO

1. Debbie, e-mail to author, August 3, 2005.
2. E. C., e-mail to author, August 8, 2005.
3. Michael Shermer, "Deconstructing the Dead: Cross Over One Last Time to Expose Medium John Edward," www.meta-religion.com/Paranormale/Skeptics/deconstructing_the_dead.htm; also see information on James Van Praagh at http://www.skepdic.com/vanpraagh.html.
4. This happened spontaneously, perhaps due to my many years of Eastern meditation.

14: THE OUIJA BOARD: DIALING FOR DANGER?

1. A. B., undated e-mail to author.
2. Anonymous e-mail to author, February 24, 2003.
3. Joanna, e-mail to author, August 12, 2005.
4. Jane Roberts, *Seth Speaks* (New York: Bantam Books, 1972), vii.
5. Stoker Hunt, *Ouija, The Most Dangerous Game* (New York: Harper & Row, 1985), 4; Edmond C. Gruss, *The Ouija Board: A Doorway to the Occult* (Phillipsburg, NJ: P & R, 1994), 9–10.
6. Hunt, 4–5; Gruss, 12.
7. Gruss, 13.
8. Ibid., 13, 15; Hunt, 5.
9. Gruss, 18.
10. Ibid.; Hunt, 5.
11. Gruss, 21.
12. Ibid., 25; Hunt, 6.
13. Hunt, 54, 57.
14. Ibid., 57.
15. Ibid., 54, 57.
16. Ibid., 59.
17. Ibid., 60.
18. Religioscope, "From Pagan Resurgence to Pagan Global

Culture, Interview with Selena Fox" August 9, 2005,
http://religion.info/english/interviews/article_186.shtml.
19. Ibid., 62.

15: AURAS, THE ASTRAL PLANE, ASTRAL TRAVEL, ENERGY, AND SYMBOLS

1. V. S., e-mail to author, August 11, 2002.
2. Matt (a teen into practicing magic), December 1, 2003.
3. http://en.wikipedia.org/wiki/Halo; http://www.arthistoryclub.com/art_history/Halo.
4. Guiley, *Encyclopedia of the Mystical & Paranormal*, 420.
5. "Troop Believers," *Washington Post*, C-1, May 13, 2002.
6. TWOT, vol. 1, 279.
7. TWOT, 280.
8. Books I have found helpful with symbols include Jean Chevalier and Alain Gheerbrant, *The Penguin Dictionary of Symbols* (Penguin Books, 1996); Jack Tresidder, *Dictionary of Symbols* (Chronicle Books, 1998); Hans Biedermann, *Dictionary of Symbolism* (Trans. copy by Facts on File, 1998); and J. C. Cooper, *An Illustrated Encyclopaedia of Traditional Symbols* (London: Thames and Hudson, 1978; paperback reprint edition, New York: Thames and Hudson, 1998).

16: TAKING A STAND: THE FEAR OF GOD IS THE BEGINNING OF WISDOM

1. Aside from Scripture quoted at the beginning of the chapter, see Proverbs 1:7; 1:29; 2:5; 10:27; 12:17; 14:26; 15:16, 33; 16:6; 19:23; 22:4; Isaiah 11:2–3; 33:6; Acts 9:31.

17: Responding to Objections

1. Alex, e-mail to author, September 27, 2002.
2. Norman L. Geisler, *False Gods of Our Time* (Eugene, OR: Harvest House, 1985), 108.

18: Protecting and Equipping Your Kids

1. Some books I recommend for this are: *The Case for Christ* and *The Case for Faith*, both by Lee Strobel; *True for You, But Not for Me*, Paul Copan; *How to Stay Christian in College*, J. Budziszewski; *The Universe Next Door*, James W. Sire; *Encyclopedia of Bible Difficulties*, Gleason Archer; *When Skeptics Ask*, Norman Geisler and Ronald M. Brooks; and *When Critics Ask*, Norman Geisler and Thomas Howe.
2. More verses on truth from Jesus Christ: John 1:14, 17; 8:32, 45–46; and 17:19.

ABOUT THE AUTHOR

Marcia Montenegro, who trusted Christ in December 1990, is a former professional astrologer, past president of the Metropolitan Astrological Society, past chairperson of the Board of Atlanta Astrology Examiners, and taught astrology for over five years. For most of her adult life, she was also involved in Eastern, New Age, and occult beliefs.

As part of her ministry, CANA/Christian Answers for the New Age, she has lectured on the New Age and occult around the country, been a guest on radio programs, published articles in Christian periodicals, and been interviewed by both secular and Christian news media. She serves with Fellowship International Mission, Allentown, PA, and is working toward a degree from Southern Evangelical Seminary, Charlotte, NC. The mother of one adult son, she lives in Arlington, VA.